WALKING
PRAGUE

WALKING
PRAGUE
THE BEST OF THE CITY

Will Tizard

NATIONAL GEOGRAPHIC

Washington, D.C.

WALKING
PRAGUE

CONTENTS

PART 1

PAGE 12
WHIRLWIND TOURS

PART 2

PAGE 46
PRAGUE'S NEIGHBORHOODS

PART 3

PAGE 170
TRAVEL ESSENTIALS

Previous pages: Old Town Square; left: Prague Castle; right: the Madonna of Dolní Kalná in the Convent of St. Agnes; above right: the Old Town Square's Astronomical Clock; bottom right: a detail from Mucha's stained-glass window in St. Vitus's Cathedral

Introduction

moved to Prague more than 20 years ago. My earliest memories of the city are intimately tied to walking. These were my extended-student years, when I was an editor at the fledgling *Prague Post,* and most of the reporters were recent college grads. In the evenings, after we'd put the paper to rest, we'd seek out the latest pub or club. New places were popping up all the time, and invariably these were located in some far-flung neighborhood. We'd set out on foot. Afterward, we might try to negotiate a night tram home, but it was usually easier and more pleasant to wander back in the darkness. Prague was built to a human scale. Its proportions were limited by the transport technologies of the 14th century: horse carts and shoe leather. Today, while the city has trams and a Metro, walking is still the most inspiring, and often quickest, way of getting around. This is especially true of Staré Město (Old Town), where the tiny passageways and alleyways, paved in shiny cobblestones, are off-limits to cars. From here, take a stroll across Charles Bridge and then climb the hill to the castle. I walk this stretch often and it always reminds me why I chose to live here. This guide will help you make the most of your stay in this medieval metropolis—a city created for walkers.

Art nouveau decoration covers the neo-Renaissance Storch House on Staré Město's Old Town Square.

Mark Baker
Longtime Prague resident, travel writer, and contributor to National Geographic Traveler *magazine*

Visiting Prague

With buildings representing 1,000 years of history and old, unspoiled streets displaying every era of European architecture from Gothic to contemporary, Prague brims with fascinating sights. Add in its busy music scene ranging from classical to avant garde, its galleries, cafés, and pubs, and the city has something for everyone.

Prague in a Nutshell

Prague's historic center consists of five districts divided by the Vltava River. Hradčany (Castle District) and the quiet streets of Malá Strana (Lesser Quarter) lie on the river's west bank; Josefov (the former Jewish quarter), Staré Město (Old Town), and Nové Město (New Town) are on the east bank. On a bend in the river to the north of Josefov, the former industrial district of Holešovice hums with modern art galleries, leafy parks, and a lively club scene that attract increasing numbers of visitors.

Navigating Prague

Prague could have been designed for walkers. Its central districts cover a relatively small area and most of the main sites are within walking distance of each other. And, except in the web of little streets around Old Town

Prague Day-by-Day

Monday Prague Castle, the Strahov Monastery, the Loreto, and most churches are open. Most other sites, including the Lobkowicz Palace at Prague Castle, are closed.

Tuesday Most sites are open. The National Museum is closed on the first Tuesday of the month. The Museum of Decorative Arts is free on Tuesday evenings.

Wednesday All sites are open. The Kampa Museum is free on the first Wednesday of the month; National Gallery sites are free from 3 p.m. to 8 p.m.; the Lobkowicz Palace is free from 4 p.m. to 6 p.m.

Thursday All sites are open.

Friday All sites are open. The National Technical Museum is free on the first Friday of each month. The Old-New Synagogue closes an hour before Shabbat.

Saturday The Jewish Museum and other Jewish sites are closed. Other sites are open.

Sunday All sites are open.

Prague is a city of great views, such as this one across Malá Strana to St. Vitus's Cathedral.

Square (Staroměstské náměstí), you are unlikely to get lost. Nonetheless, it is a good idea to arm yourself with a detailed street map. You can get a good idea of the city's layout from a trip up one of its many towers. Almost all the city's landmarks will be in view, and you'll be able to see the main thoroughfares that link them.

Prague has two house-numbering systems, and both numbers appear on the outsides of some buildings. Numbers on a red background belong to the old, or "descriptive," system for registering buildings in the city records, initiated in the 18th century. Numbers on a blue background belong to the "new" system of numbering buildings sequentially in a street that was introduced in the 19th century. This book uses the new system so look for the blue plates.

Enjoying Prague for Less

Admission fees are not particularly high in Prague, but you can cut costs by purchasing a Prague Card, which provides free or discounted entry to many museums and historic buildings. The card also qualifies you for discounts on some organized tours and river cruises. You can also buy twenty-four-hour and three-day public transport passes.

Using This Guide

Each tour—which might be only a walk, or might take advantage of the city's public transportation as well—is plotted on a map and has been planned to take into account opening hours and the times of day when sites are less crowded. Many end near restaurants or lively nightspots for evening activities.

Whirlwind Tours

Whirlwind Tours are for people who have only a day or weekend and want to be sure that they see the best. Choose a tour based on your time and interests: One Day; Weekend (Day 1 & Day 2); For Fun; For History Lovers; For Art Nouveau & Cubism; and With Kids (Day 1 & Day 2).

Tips For the Day and Weekend Tours, a Tips spread following the itinerary map provides insider information on detours from the key sites, extra places to see, nearby cafés and restaurants, and ideas for adapting the tours to suit your interests.

Site Descriptions

In the For Fun, History Lovers, Art Nouveau & Cubism, and With Kids tours, key sites spreads following the maps provide descriptions of all the sites and practical information for visitors.

Neighborhood Tours

The six neighborhood tours each begin with an introduction, followed by an itinerary map highlighting the key sites that make up the tour and detailed key sites descriptions. Each tour is followed by an "in-depth" spread showcasing one major site along the route, a "distinctly" Prague spread providing background information on a quintessential element of that neighborhood, and a "best of" spread that groups sites thematically.

Itinerary Map A map of the neighborhood shows the locations of the key sites, Metro stations, and main streets.

Captions These blurbs briefly describe the key sites and give instructions on finding the next site on the tour. Page references direct you to full descriptions of the sites on the following pages.

Route

Key Sites Descriptions These spreads provide a detailed description and highlights for each site, following the order on the map, plus its address, website, phone number, entrance fee, days closed, and nearest Metro and tram stops.

Good Eats Refer to these lists for a selection of cafés and restaurants along the tour.

Price Ranges for Key Sites

$	Less than $8
$$	$8–$16
$$$	$16–$24
$$$$	$24–30
$$$$$	More than $30

Price Ranges for Good Eats
(for one person, excluding drinks)

$	Less than $10
$$	$10–$15
$$$	$15–$25
$$$$	$25–$35
$$$$$	More than $35

PART 1

Whirlwind Tours

Prague in a Day

Pack 1,000 years of history into one day.

MARIÁNSKÉ HRADBY

KRÁLOVSKÁ
ZAHRADA

CHOTK

HRADČANY

Arcibiskupský
palác

Prague Castle
(Pražský hrad)

KLA

⑥

Bazilika sv. Jiří

Chrám
sv. Víta

Malostranská

HRADČANSKÉ
NÁMĚSTÍ

Valdštejnsk
palác

NERUDOVA

Church of St. Nichola
(Kostel sv. Mikuláše)

Schönbornský
palác

⑤

KARMELITSKÁ

SCHÖNBORNSKÁ
ZAHRADA

Kostel
Panny
Marie
Vítězné

MALTÉZSKÉ
NÁMĚSTÍ

Kamp

MALÁ STRANA

LOBKOVICKÁ
ZAHRADA

Nostický
palác

Čertovka

Zrcadlové
bludiště

SEMINÁŘSKÁ
ZAHRADA

ÚJEZD

VÍTĚZNÁ

⑤ **Church of St. Nicholas** (see
pp. 99–100) This high-baroque
gem designed by father-and-son
team Christoph and Kilian Ignatz
Dientzenhofer is festooned with feats
of technical mastery. Its stunning tower
forms the signature icon of Prague's
Malá Strana district. Walk west on
Nerudova and turn onto Ke Hradu.

⑥ **Prague Castle** (see pp. 118–124)
One of Europe's grandest castles
has three courtyards around which
are ranged palaces, galleries,
gardens, museums, a Romanesque
basilica, and the magnificent
St. Vitus's Cathedral.

PRAGUE IN A DAY   DISTANCE: 2 MILES (3.2 KM)
TIME: APPROX. 8 HOURS   METRO START: MUZEUM, MŮSTEK

4 Charles Bridge (see pp. 54–55)
Construction of this timeless stone bridge began around 1357. It is the only bridge in the city reserved solely for walkers. Head west on Mostecká.

400 meters
400 yards

Kláster sv. Anežký České

JOSEFOV

Španělská synagoga

HAŠTALSKÉ NÁMĚSTÍ

Rudolfinum

UPM
STARÝ
ŽIDOVSKÝ
HŘBITOV

Vysoká synagoga

DLOUHÁ

MÁNESŮV MOST

Pinkasova synagoga

sv. Jakub
Municipal House
(Obecní dům)

NÁMĚSTÍ
REPUBLIKY

Staroměstská

Kostel sv. Mikuláše

2

Náměstí
Republiky

arles Bridge
(árlův most)

Klementinum

CELETNÁ

HYBERNSKÁ

4

3
Old Town Square
(Staroměstské náměstí)

Prašná brána

KARLOVA

Muzeum
Bedřicha
Smetany

STARÉ MĚSTO

Stavovské
divadlo

Můstek

NA PŘÍKOPĚ

Muchovo
muzeum

Betlémská
kaple

UHELNÝ
TRH

3 Old Town Square (see
pp. 62–65) Every style of
architecture that Prague has
to offer—from Gothic through
baroque and beyond—line this
historic former market square at
the heart of Staré Město. Follow
Karlova four blocks west.

Střelecký
ostrov

sv. Kříž

NÁRODNÍ

Café Slavia

Palác
Adria

MOST LEGIÍ

Národní
divadlo

1
Wenceslas Square
(Václavské náměstí)

Kostel
Panny
Marie
Sněžné

Můstek

Národní
třída

Muzeum

2 Municipal House (see
pp. 59–60) Step back in time at this
ornate art nouveau showpiece with
its old-Vienna-style coffeehouse.
Follow Celetná four blocks west.

1 Wenceslas Square
(see p. 140) This
half-mile-long (1 km)
boulevard is the place
where the crowds
gathered to demand
freedom in 1989. Now
it's the best spot to
check the pulse of
21st-century Prague.
Turn right at the
northern end onto
Na Příkopě.

Central Prague
Area enlarged above

WHIRLWIND TOURS

Tips

The best of the best sites are easy to tour in a day. The page references below will guide you to detailed information elsewhere in the book. If you are short of time or the queues are long, alternative ticketing options and historic cafés provide easy ways to see these attractions and soak up the atmosphere.

❶ Wenceslas Square (see p. 140)
For a good view of Wenceslas Square (Václavské náměstí) stand at the top end in front of the National Museum (Národní muzeum). ■ **Mysak,** just off the square on Vodičkova *(No. 31),* is a restored pre-World War II gem of a café with floor mosaics, wooden alcoves, and a marble staircase. It offers

A copper dome and a large mosaic top Municipal House's ornately decorated exterior.

a selection of cakes with classic espresso to go with its fine people-watching possibilities. ■ **Jama** *(V Jáma 7)* is an ever popular expat burger bar that's a hit with the locals.

❷ Municipal House (see pp. 59–60)
If no tours of Municipal House (Obecní dům) are available on the day you visit, you can still soak up the building's fin-de-siècle atmosphere in the ground-floor ■ **Municipal House Café** while a pianist tinkles the ivories.

❸ Old Town Square (see pp. 62–65)
From the top of the ■ **Old Town Hall Tower** on the west side of Old Town Square (Staroměstské náměstí) you have a bird's-eye view of all the activity going on in the square below as well as of every major landmark in the city. Thanks to a clever relay-system of elevators, the climb is not as challenging as it looks. The tower

is open in winter, too, unlike many others in the city. In March and December, the square hosts holiday markets with mulled wine on offer that's guaranteed to warm you up fast.

Heading southwest to Karlova, you'll come to ■ **MALÉ NÁMĚSTÍ,** a quiet little square with restaurant tables on the sidewalk. In the middle of the square is Prague's oldest surviving fountain, dating from 1560. You can see the date on its metalwork grille.

❹ Charles Bridge (see pp. 54–55)
If the summer crowds on Charles Bridge (Karlův most) are overwhelming, you might find solace out on the Vltava River itself, which you can reach with a ■ **ROWBOAT RENTAL** from the moorings at Novotného lávka *(www .lavka.cz),* south of the bridge on the Staré Město side, beside the Smetana Museum (Muzeum Bedřicha Smetany).

❺ Church of St. Nicholas (see pp. 99–100) Probably the best way to experience the majesty of the almost overwhelming confection of baroque flourishes inside Malá Strana's Church of St. Nicholas (Kostel sv. Mikuláše) is when the organ is thundering out some ancient hymn. A concert schedule is regularly updated on the church website *(www.stnicholas.cz)* and performances are affordable.

CUSTOMIZING **YOUR DAY**

If you want to make sure you have plenty of time to spend at Prague Castle, you could start there. Arrive just before 9 a.m. to beat the queues. This will give you enough time to take the longest tour if you want. You can then follow the rest of this tour in reverse, ending at Wenceslas Square, or at Municipal House, where you can enjoy a concert or a meal.

❻ Prague Castle (see pp. 118–124)
The city's most epic sight, Prague Castle (Pražský hrad) is spread over an extensive area. You won't have time to see much of it on a one-day tour of the city, but at the very least you can enter through the stately west gate and wander around the courtyards for free, adding a stroll through its grand gardens in summer. Buy a Circuit B ticket to see the most popular buildings.

The ■ **LOBKOWICZ PALACE CAFÉ** in the castle complex serves light meals and has a terrace with a great view. A reliable eating spot near the castle is the local artists' hangout ■ **U ZAVĚŠENÝHO KAFE** *(Úvoz 6).* For the quickest route down to Malá Strana and a fabulous view, take the ■ **OLD CASTLE STEPS** (Staré zámecké schody) from the castle exit at the eastern end of Jiřská. This will bring you out near the Malostranská Metro station.

WHIRLWIND TOURS

Prague in a Weekend

A medieval castle, baroque churches, quiet waterside streets, and one of the city's main shopping areas are on the first day's tour.

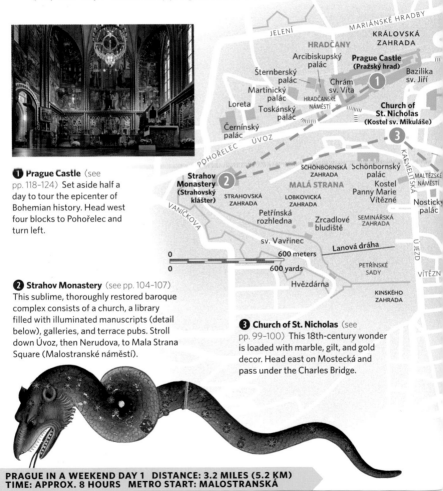

WHIRLWIND TOURS

1 Prague Castle (see pp. 118–124) Set aside half a day to tour the epicenter of Bohemian history. Head west four blocks to Pohořelec and turn left.

2 Strahov Monastery (see pp. 104–107) This sublime, thoroughly restored baroque complex consists of a church, a library filled with illuminated manuscripts (detail below), galleries, and terrace pubs. Stroll down Úvoz, then Nerudova, to Mala Strana Square (Malostranské náměstí).

3 Church of St. Nicholas (see pp. 99–100) This 18th-century wonder is loaded with marble, gilt, and gold decor. Head east on Mostecká and pass under the Charles Bridge.

Map labels:
JELENÍ
MARIÁNSKÉ HRADBY
HRADČANY
KRÁLOVSKÁ ZAHRADA
Arcibiskupský palác
Prague Castle (Pražský hrad)
Šternberský palác
Chrám sv. Víta
Bazilika sv. Jiří
Martinický palác
Loreta
HRADČANSKÉ NÁMĚSTÍ
Toskánský palác
Church of St. Nicholas (Kostel sv. Mikuláše)
Černínský palác
ÚVOZ
POHOŘELEC
KARMELITSKÁ
Strahov Monastery (Strahovský klášter)
SCHÖNBORNSKÁ ZAHRADA
Schönbornský palác
MALTÉZSKÉ NÁMĚSTÍ
STRAHOVSKÁ ZAHRADA
MALÁ STRANA
Kostel Panny Marie Vítězné
LOBKOVICKÁ ZAHRADA
VANIČKOVA
Petřínská rozhledna
Zrcadlové bludiště
SEMINÁŘSKÁ ZAHRADA
Nosticky palác
sv. Vavřinec
Lanová dráha
ÚJEZD
0 600 meters
0 600 yards
PETŘÍNSKÉ SADY
VÍTĚZN
Hvězdárna
KINSKÉHO ZAHRADA

PRAGUE IN A WEEKEND DAY 1   DISTANCE: 3.2 MILES (5.2 KM)
TIME: APPROX. 8 HOURS   METRO START: MALOSTRANSKÁ

6 Wenceslas Square (see p. 140) After taking in the eclectic architecture, from art nouveau to modernist, indulge in a spot of shopping or stop for a drink or coffee in one of the many cafés.

U BRUSKÝCH KASÁREN
KLÁROV
Malostranská
Valdštejnský palác
MÁNESŮV MOST
Rudolfinum
UPM
PAŘÍŽSKÁ
17 LISTOPADU
STARÝ ŽIDOVSKÝ HŘBITOV
Španělská synagoga
Vysoká synagoga
DLOUHÁ
Pinkasova synagoga
Staroměstská
Kostel sv. Mikuláše
Klementinum
MARIÁNSKÉ NÁMĚSTÍ
Chrám Matky Boží před Týnem
sv. Jakub
UNGELT
Obecní dům
CELETNÁ
Náměstí Republiky
CHARLES BRIDGE (KARLŮV MOST)
STAROMĚSTSKÉ NÁMĚSTÍ
Staroměstská radnice
KARLOVA
Karolinum
NA PŘÍKOPĚ
Kampa Island
ABŘEŽÍ
STARÉ MĚSTO
Stavovské divadlo
Muchovo muzeum
JINDŘIŠSKÁ
Muzeum Bedřicha Smetany
SMETANOVO NÁBŘEŽÍ
Betlémská kaple
sv. Kříž
UHELNÝ TRH
Kostel Panny Marie Sněžné
Můstek
VÁCLAVSKÉ
Můstek
Střelecký ostrov
MOST LEGIÍ
Vltava
Café Slavia
NÁRODNÍ
Palác Adria
WENCESLAS SQUARE
(VÁCLAVSKÉ NÁMĚSTÍ)
5 National Theater
(Národní divadlo)
SPÁLENÁ
Národní třída
Wenceslas Square
(Václavské náměstí)
Dům Diamant
Novoměstská radnice
ŠTĚPÁNSKÁ
Muzeum
ŽITNÁ

5 National Theater (see p. 145) This dignified performance hall demonstrates the importance of the stage (*divadlo*) in Bohemian consciousness. Walk five blocks east on Národní.

4 Kampa Island (see p. 102) With pretty waterside streets, an attractive park, and a modern art gallery, this is a good place to relax. Stroll across Legionnaire's Bridge (Most Legií).

Central Prague
Area enlarged above

WHIRLWIND TOURS

Tips

All the destinations are described in detail elsewhere in the book—just follow the cross-references for more information. These tips provide advice on customizing your visits to fit in with your interests if you are short of time and suggestions for alternative sites and places to eat.

WHIRLWIND TOURS

❶ Prague Castle (see pp. 118–124) The terrace café in the privately owned ■ **LOBKOWICZ PALACE** (Lobkovický palác; see pp. 128–129) within the castle complex is a good place to start the day. If the surfeit of sights at the world's largest castle complex seems overwhelming, concentrate on the aspect that interests you. Art lovers, for

St. Norbert's restaurant is near the main entrance to the Strahov Monastery.

example, can concentrate on ■ **PRAGUE CASTLE PICTURE GALLERY** (Obrazárna Pražského hradu; see p. 118) or buy a Circuit C ticket, which also includes the treasury of St. Vitus's Cathedral. Architecture mavens must see the ■ **VLADISLAV HALL** in the Old Royal Palace (Starý královský palác; see pp. 118–119). Lovers of the cute should head for ■ **GOLDEN LANE** (Zlatá ulička; see pp. 123–124).

❷ Strahov Monastery (see pp. 104–107) The restored art collections at the Strahov Monastery (Strahovský klášter) are inspiring to see, but so are the views from this hilltop perch. The St. Norbert brew, which was first created by monks several centuries ago, has a good hoppy flavor. You'll find it in the ■ **KLÁŠTERNI PIVOVAR STRAHOV** café beside the Gallery Miro at the main entrance.

❸ Church of St. Nicholas (see pp. 99–100) The postcard-perfect Church of St. Nicholas (Kostel sv. Mikuláše) is surrounded by several more earthy institutions. One such place beloved by locals is ■ **U GLAUBICŮ** (*Malostranské náměstí 5*), which has outdoor tables on the sidewalk as well as several seating areas inside.

❹ Kampa Island (see p. 102) The park beside the Vltava River has plenty of benches and extensive lawns, making it a good spot for a picnic. The ■ **KAMPA MUSEUM** (see pp. 102, 167) features important modern Czech art. At the northern end of the island, hundreds of conceptual artists appear to have taken over the bridge by Grand Burgrave's, attaching padlocks to the wrought-iron railing as testaments to eternal love.

❺ National Theater (see p. 145) The area around the National Theater (Národní divadlo) abounds in great options for restoring body and spirits, the best known of which is ■ **CAFÉ SLAVIA** (see p. 71) on Smetanovo nábřeží, just opposite the theater. Playwright and former president Václav Havel and pals once broke in just to keep the beer flowing, so lauded is the café's history as a refuge for writers. Leo Tolstoy, another

---

CUSTOMIZING **YOUR DAY**

If you're a fan of contemporary art you can add in some works by Czech artist David Černý on this walk. In the garden of the German embassy on Vlašská (*No. 19*), you can see "Quo Vadis," a golden Trabant car on legs, tribute to the 4,000 East Germans who arrived in their Trabants in 1989. Outside the Kafka Museum (see p. 97), a short distance east of the Church of St. Nicholas, is "Streams," consisting of statues of two men urinating into a pool in the shape of the Czech Republic. Pop into the Lucerna Passage (see p. 141) off Wenceslas Square to find Černý's upside-down statue of St. Wenceslas on his horse.

---

customer in his day, would surely have approved.

❻ Wenceslas Square (see p. 140) This broad promenade combines great architecture and retail therapy. The ■ **BAT'A** shoe store (*No. 6*) occupies one of Prague's finest functionalist buildings. Its sleek glass-and-steel form makes choosing a pair of classic Czech walking shoes a true joy. Shopping opportunities continue on ■ **NA PŘÍKOPĚ,** which runs east from Wenceslas Square. And look out for ■ **NEKÁZANKA,** a little street off to the right. Two ornate enclosed bridges modeled on Venice's Bridge of Sighs span the street at second-floor level.

Prague in a Weekend

Explore Prague's extensive old Jewish quarter, followed by its medieval center, and finish with icons of cubist and baroque architecture.

1 **Jewish Museum** (see pp. 77–83) Six historic sites—survivors of the ghetto clearance in the early 20th century—make up the museum. The oldest Gothic synagogue in Central Europe, the Old-New, stands nearby. Head south on Pařížská to Old Town Square.

2 **Old Town Square** (see pp. 62–65) Every street in Staré Město (Old Town) seems to lead to this medieval-era plaza. Aside from steady crowds and a monument to the nation's great martyr, Jan Hus, the square hosts yearlong events, galas, and craft stalls. Head east on Štupartská.

PRAGUE IN A WEEKEND DAY 2   DISTANCE: 1.2 MILES (2 KM)
TIME: APPROX. 8 HOURS   METRO START: STAROMĚSTSKÁ

❺ Estates Theater (see p. 61) This baroque opera house, its auditorium ringed with wrought-iron balconies, is the place where Wolfgang Amadeus Mozart conducted two of his operas in the late 1700s.

❹ House of the Black Madonna (see p. 60) The city's finest example of the native Czech innovation of cubist architecture, this former 1920s' department store can be enjoyed from the terrace café upstairs. Cross Ovocný trh to the southwest.

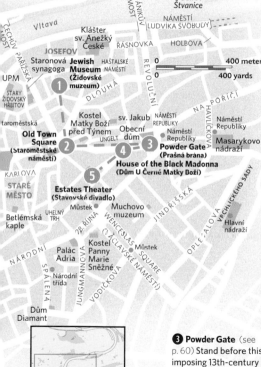

Vltava

ŠTEFÁNIKŮV MOST

Ostrov Štvanice

NÁMĚSTÍ LUDVÍKA SVOBODY

Klášter sv. Anežky České

RÁSNOVKA

HOLBOVÁ

ČECHŮV MOST

PAŘÍŽSKÁ

JOSEFOV

Staronová synagoga

Jewish Museum (Židovské muzeum) ①

HAŠTALSKÉ NÁMĚSTÍ

REVOLUČNÍ

0   400 meters
0   400 yards

UPM

STARÝ ŽIDOVSKÝ HŘBITOV

DLOUHÁ

NA POŘÍČÍ

taroměstská

Kostel Matky Boží před Týnem

sv. Jakub

NÁMĚSTÍ REPUBLIKY

HAVLÍČKOVA

Náměstí Republiky

Old Town Square (Staroměstské náměstí) ②

Obecní dům

UNGELT

Náměstí Republiky

Masarykovo nádraží

Powder Gate (Prašná brána) ③

House of the Black Madonna (Dům U Černé Matky Boží) ④

KARLOVA

STARÉ MĚSTO

Estates Theater (Stavovské divadlo) ⑤

Muštek

UHELNÝ TRH

Muchovo muzeum

JINDŘIŠSKÁ

VRCHLICKÉHO SADY

OPLETALOVÁ

Hlavní nádraží

Betlémská kaple

28. ŘÍJNA

Hlavní nádraží

NÁRODNÍ

Palác Adria

Kostel Panny Marie Sněžné

Muštek

VÁCLAVSKÉ NÁMĚSTÍ

WENCESLAS SQUARE (VÁCLAVSKÉ NÁMĚSTÍ)

ŠPÁLENÁ

JUNGMANNOVA

Národní třída

VODIČKOVA

Dům Diamant

Central Prague
Area enlarged above

❸ Powder Gate (see p. 60) Stand before this imposing 13th-century stone archway, one of the original gates in the city wall that ringed Staré Město to keep out invaders. Go one block west on Celetná.

Tips

You'll find detailed write-ups on these sites in the neighborhood chapters; just follow the page references. The tips below include alternative suggestions for avoiding the crowds and for tailoring the tour to suit your own interests, together with information on cafés and restaurants for refreshment stops.

WHIRLWIND TOURS

❶ Jewish Museum (see pp. 77–83) Allow half a day to look around the Jewish Museum (Židovské muzeum). If you're feeling peckish, try ■ **BAKESHOP PRAHA** (*Kozí 1, www.bakeshop.cz, 222 316 823, $–$$*) near the Spanish Synagogue (Španělská synagoga; see pp. 82–83). This large, bright bakery with a difference serves bagels and croissants, soups, salads, sandwiches, and sweet pastries. Outside the Spanish Synagogue, you can see a ■ **MONUMENT**

The interior of the Old-New Synagogue

TO FRANZ KAFKA. At the top of Pařížská, close to the Old-New Synagogue (Staronová synagoga) is a striking, bow fronted, art nouveau building topped by a tall, Gothic-style tower. It houses the ■ **CANTINETTA FIORENTINA** (*Pařížská 98, www.cantinetta.cz, 222 326 203, $$$–$$$$$*), serving Italian food in an equally stylish art nouveau interior.

❷ Old Town Square (see pp. 62–65) Tucked away in a quiet little courtyard behind the Church of Our Lady Before Týn (Kostel Matky Boží před Tynem) is one of the city's best bookstores for lovers of Czech art and letters, the ■ **TÝNSKÁ LITERÁRNÍ KAVÁRNA,** or literary café (*Týnská 6, 224 827 807*). Also on the courtyard is the ■ **HOUSE AT THE GOLDEN RING** (Dům U Zlatého Prstenu; *Týnská 6, www.citygalleryprague. cz, 224 827 022–024, $, closed Mon.*).

Run by City Gallery Prague, this art trove has a permanent collection of Czech 20th-century art and also puts on temporary exhibitions of work by emerging local artists. With tables and chairs in the shade, the courtyard itself provides a secluded spot for a rest away from the crowds on Old Town Square.

❸ Powder Gate (see p. 60) Don't overlook the imposing neoclassical facade opposite the Powder Gate (Prašná brána) even though it looks at first blush like just another shopping mall. ■ SLOVANSKÝ DŮM (Slavic House, formerly known as Vernierov Palace; *Na Příkopě 22, www.wlovanskydum.cz, 221 451 380)* was built in 1695 and has a remodeled facade dating from 1797. For several years following the Velvet Revolution, the building was a seedy hangout for addicts and teens. Now it's the place to see a big-screen film at Cinema City, buy a designer suit in one of the many stores, or grab a Mediterranean lunch at Kogo restaurant *(www.kogo.cz, 21 451 258/259, $$$–$$$$$).*

❹ House of the Black Madonna (see p. 60) The ■ KUBISTA shop on the ground floor of the House of the Black Madonna (Dům U Černé Matky Boží) carries on the tradition that dates from the building's earlier incarnation

CUSTOMIZING **YOUR DAY**

The ground floor of the Old Town Hall in Old Town Square houses Prague's largest Tourist Information Center, which provides general information on the city and sells theater and concert tickets. It's an excellent place to pick up details on the wealth of small concerts held in the city's many churches and museums (see p. 69). Most concerts take place in the early evening and last about an hour, and you can usually buy tickets on the door.

as a department store. Cubist china, decor, and furniture you wouldn't find anywhere else make tempting gifts.

❺ Estates Theater (see p. 61) The bronze statue of a hollow cloaked figure at the front of the Estates Theater (Stavovské divadlo), titled ■ CLOAK OF CONSCIENCE, is one of a series by Czech sculptor Anna Chromý. Just opposite the theater, the ■ CAROLINUM (Karolinum; *Ovocný trh 3)* is one of the oldest buildings of Prague University, founded by Emperor Charles IV in 1348. Regular exhibitions go up in the art gallery in the south wing of the ground floor. The annual World Press Photo touring exhibition *(www.worldpressphoto.org)*, which visits Prague in early fall each year, is one of the most popular events held here.

Prague for Fun

From modern art to a sky-high cocktail bar via luxury shopping and a river cruise, Prague has plenty to satisfy hedonists.

❺ Žižkov TV Tower (see p. 29) Ascend the tower for cocktails in the most unusual and panoramic bar in town.

❹ Vltava River Cruise (see p. 29) Enjoy a crowd-free view of some of Prague's finest sights on a round-trip river cruise. Walk a block south and catch tram 10 to the Perunova stop. Then walk six blocks north.

MILADY HORÁKO

Hradčanská

0   1000 meters
0   1000 yards

JELENÍ

PATOČKOVA

Chrám sv. Víta   Bazilika sv. Jiří
Malostranská   Rudolfinu
Starý královský palác   Valdštejnský   MÁNESŮV
palác   MOST
Kostel sv.   Staroměstsk
Strahovský   Mikuláše
klášter   Karlův most
   Kostel   **Vltava**
   Panny   **River Cruise** ❹
   Marie
   Vítězné

❸ U Medvídků (see p. 28) A seven-century-long pedigree is impressive even for a Czech pub. This one has earned its accolades—plus a reputation among locals for freshly tapped lager and a menu of Bohemian traditional pub grub at its best. Walk three blocks west to the river and catch tram 17 south to Rašínovo nábřeží.

MOST
LEGIÍ
Národní
divadlo

JIRÁSKŮV
MOST

Karlo
náměs

PRAGUE FOR FUN   DISTANCE: 5.5 MILES (8.9 KM)
TIME: 10 HOURS   METRO START: VLTAVSKÁ

① Veletržní Palace (see pp. 28, 162–163) Drift through the former Trade Fair Palace, which holds Alphons Mucha's greatest work, the Slav Epic, modern art from all over Europe, and no shortage of retro Czech designs, from typewriters to art nouveau stained glass. Catch tram 17 to the Právnická fakulta stop in Staré Město.

② Pařížská (see p. 28) This glitzy, three-block shopping street in Staré Město is the place to spy the latest trends in international haute couture. Walk across Old Town Square (Staroměstské náměstí), turn right at the Astronomical Clock, and follow Jilská south three blocks to Na Perštýně.

Planetárium Praha

STROJNICKÁ

BUBENSKÁ

VELETRŽNÍ

KORUNOVAČNÍ

① Veletržní Palace (Veletržní palác)

Vltavská

Národní Technické muzeum

NÁBŘEŽÍ EDVARDA BENEŠE

LETNÁ PARK (LETENSKÉ SADY)

HLÁVKŮV MOST

DVOŘÁKOVO NÁBŘEŽÍ

ČECHŮV MOST

Klášter sv. Anežky České

② Pařížská

KE ŠTVANICI

Židovské muzeum

Florenc

③ U Medvídků

Kostel sv. Jakuba

Clam-Gallasův palác

Obecní dům & Prašná brána

Klementinum

Dům U Černé Matky Boží

Stavovské divadlo

Hlavní nádraží

Betlémská kaple

Hlavní nádraží

Müstek

Žižkov TV Tower

Národní třída

Lucerna Passage

ITALSKÁ

SLAVÍKOVA

ONDŘÍČKOVA

⑤ ŽIŽKOV

JIČÍNSKÁ

Muzeum

RIEGROVY SADY

Karlovo náměstí

Národní muzeum

Jiřího z Poděbrad

Flora

VINOHRADSKÁ

Kostel sv. Cyrila a Metoděje

JEČNÁ

Karlovo náměstí

NOVÉ MĚSTO

GOOD **EATS**

■ LA CASA BLŮ

A Pařížská location may price lunch in the stratosphere, but this bar just two blocks away serves affordable, authentic Mexican food. **Kozí 15, Prague 1, 224 818 270, $**

■ LOKÁL

A hit among fussy Praguers for its simple retro style and authentic old Czech recipes, this comforting, clean-lined pub also serves unpasteurized, full-flavor beer kept in special new tanks. **Dlouhá 33, Prague 1, 222 316 265, $**

■ NOSTRESS

This stylish little café indulges its patrons with tiger prawns, zesty salads, and other Mediterranean fare served in an elegant garden atmosphere. **Dušní 10, Prague 1, 222 317 007, $$**

Veletržní Palace

① For a quick overview of the collection take the glass elevator in the Small Hall, which whizzes you up past four floors of 19th- and 20th-century painting, sculpture, and design. One of the least-known, most exciting sections of the gallery is the large collection of Czech contemporary art on the second floor.

Dukelských Hrdinů 47, Prague 7 • www.ngprague.cz • 224 301 122 • $ • Closed Mon. • Metro: Vltavská • Tram: 12, 24

Pařížská

② Whether or not you feel the need to shell out for a Prada handbag, an Italian evening gown, or $450 shoes, take a walk along Pařižská (which translates as Paris Street). This broad boulevard lined with elegant art nouveau apartment buildings features Dior, Gucci, Fendi, Dolce & Gabbana, Burberry, and many more of the big names of international fashion. You can find jewelry, accessories, and Bohemian glass here as well. Or slip into one of the cafés and sip on a coffee as you enjoy the sight of fellow shoppers—some in colored fur and spike heels.

Pařížská, Prague 1 • Metro: Staroměstská • Tram: 17, 18

U Medvídků

③ Noisy and smoky, this institution among Prague's pubs has stood proud since its founding in 1466. Special tanks keep the beer at its freshest and purest. There's beer in the lunch dishes, too. The beer-basted roast beef is a special treat, as is the classic goulash and duck with potato dumplings and sauerkraut. The brass band and labyrinth of halls make a visit all the more memorable.

Na Perštýně 7, Prague 1 • 224 211 916 • Metro: Národní třída • Tram: 6, 9, 18, 22

Vltava River Cruise

4 Relax for an hour on the deck of a Prague Steamship Company river cruiser. As the city skyline drifts past, you can study the facades of waterside buildings such as the National Theater and the Smetana Museum, get a different angle on the Charles Bridge and some of the city's 17 other bridges as you pass beneath, watch Prague Castle and St. Vitus's Cathedral looming overhead, and take a good look at the fortifications built into the Vyšehrad promontory. A 90-minute cruise is also available, as are options that include coffee and dessert.

Rašínovo nábřeží, Prague 2 • www.prague steamboats.com • 224 931 013 • $$–$$$ • Closed Nov.–Feb. • Metro: Karlovo náměstí • Tram: 3, 14, 17

Žižkov TV Tower

5 Sipping gin and tonic 216 feet (66 m) above the colorful Žižkov district in this former radio-jamming station puts you eye to eye with the giant statue of the Bohemian rebel leader Jan Žižka sitting astride his steed a few blocks over on Vítkov Hill. The three-deck tower, built in the late 1980s to prevent radio broadcasts from Western Europe reaching impressionable Czechs, now transmits local TV and radio programs. A one-room hotel above the restaurant is booked up years in advance.

Mahlerovy sady 1, Prague 3 • www.towerpark.cz • 210 320 081 • $ • Metro: Jiřího z Poděbrad • Tram: 5, 9, 11, 13, 26

Several of David Černý's baby sculptures swarm up and down the Žižkov Tower.

Prague for History Lovers

Situated at the very heart of Europe, Prague bears the scars of more than 1,000 turbulent years of power struggles, wars, and occupation.

6 **Prague Castle** (see pp. 33, 118–124)
This hilltop site, watched over by the gargoyles on St. Vitus's Cathedral (below), shows traces of every local ruling power, from the pagan tribes of prehistoric times through to the current presidency of the Czech Republic.

5 **Legionnaire's Bridge** (see p. 33)
Enjoy views of the city without the crowds from this bridge, which commemorates Czech and Slovak soldiers whose actions in World War I marked a turning point in the fight for independence. Walk two blocks west to Újezd and take tram 22 to the Pohořelec stop.

4 **Vyšehrad** (see pp. 33, 143)
Walk among the ruins on this exposed hilltop where the first Bohemian ruling dynasty established a stronghold. Take tram 6 or 18 from the Albertov stop to Národní třída and walk west.

JELENÍ

PATOČKOVA

Prague Castle
(Pražský hrad)

6

Malostranská

Valdštejnský palác

Kostel sv. Mikuláše

Strahovský klášter

Karl mos

Muzeu Bedřic Smeta

Kostel Panny Marie Vítězné

VANIČKOVA

Petřínské sady

ÚJEZD

Legionnaire's Bridge
(Most Legií)   **5**

KINSKY GARDENS
(ZAHRADA KINSKÝCH)

PŘESLOVA

ZBOROVSKÁ

JIRÁSK MOS

V BOTANICE

SMÍCHOV

Anděl

VLTAVSKÁ

NADRAŽNÍ

SVORNOSTI

**PRAGUE FOR HISTORY LOVERS   DISTANCE: 3.9 MILES (6.3 KM)
TIME: 10 HOURS   METRO START: MŮSTEK**

WHIRLWIND TOURS

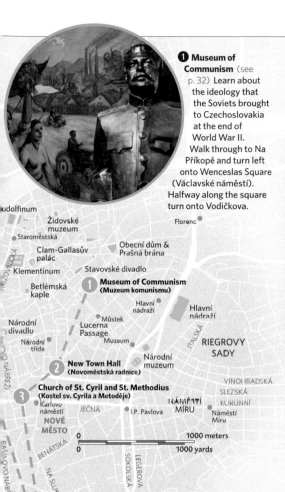

❶ Museum of Communism (see p. 32) Learn about the ideology that the Soviets brought to Czechoslovakia at the end of World War II. Walk through to Na Příkopě and turn left onto Wenceslas Square (Václavské náměstí). Halfway along the square turn onto Vodičkova.

udolfinum

Žídovské muzeum

Staroměstská

Clam-Gallasův palác

Klementinum

Betlémská kaple

Národní divadlo

Národní třída

Obecní dům & Prašná brána

Stavovské divadlo

Florenc

❶ Museum of Communism (Muzeum komunismu)

Hlavní nádraží

Hlavní nádraží

Můstek

Lucerna Passage

Muzeum

Národní muzeum

RIEGROVY SADY

❷ New Town Hall (Novoměstská radnice)

❸ Church of St. Cyril and St. Methodius (Kostel sv. Cyrila a Metoděje)

Karlovo náměstí

NOVÉ MĚSTO

JEČNÁ

I.P. Pavlova

NÁMĚSTÍ MÍRU

Náměstí Míru

VINOHRADSKÁ

SLEZSKÁ

KORUNNÍ

0   1000 meters

0   1000 yards

❹ Vyšehrad

Rotunda sv. Martina

Vyšehrad

SEKANINOVA

JAROMÍROVA

ČIKLOVA

❷ New Town Hall (see pp. 32, 141–142) See the spot where Praguers honed their political protest skills with the First Defenestration, in 1419. Walk south down Charles Square (Karlovo náměstí) and turn right onto Resslova.

❸ Church of St. Cyril and St. Methodius (see pp. 32, 142–143) Artillery scars around the entrance to the crypt mark the place where the assassins of the Nazi governor of Czechoslovakia and Moravia in World War II fought and died. A museum in the crypt tells the story. Take tram 18 or 24 to the Albertov stop.

WHIRLWIND TOURS

Museum of Communism

1 The Museum of Communism (Muzeum komunismu) explores the humiliations, lies, and general dysfunction of the communist system as it affected ordinary people's daily lives. Exhibits include political posters, film footage from the time, and mock-ups of an agitprop-filled schoolroom and a secret police listening post.

Na příkopě 10, Prague 1 ▪ www.muzeumkomunismu.cz ▪ 224 212 966 ▪ $$
▪ Metro: Můstek ▪ Tram: 6, 9, 22

New Town Hall

2 Mark the spot where Hussites (reformers wanting changes in the Catholic Church) threw a group of town councillors from the tower at the New Town Hall (Novoměstská radnice). The event sparked off the Hussite Wars in 1419.

Karlovo náměstí 1, Prague 2 ▪ www.nrpraha.cz
▪ 224 948 229 ▪ Closed Oct.–April and Mon.
▪ Metro: Karlovo náměstí ▪ Tram: 3, 6, 18, 22, 24

The museum at Sts. Cyril and Methodius commemorates the assassins of Reinhard Heydrich.

Church of St. Cyril and St. Methodius

3 A plaque on the south wall of the Church of St. Cyril and St. Methodius (Kostel sv. Cyrila a Metoděje) honors the bravery of the assassins of Nazi governor Reinhard Heydrich. Displays in the crypt provide details about the plot, the men who carried it out, and the people who helped them.

Resslova 9a, Prague 2 ▪ www.prague.net
▪ 224 920 686 ▪ $ ▪ Closed Mon. Mar.–Oct.,
Sun.–Mon. Nov.–Feb. ▪ Metro: Karlovo náměstí ▪ Tram: 3, 6, 18, 22, 24

Vyšehrad

4 Thanks to war and the tides of time, little of the original 10th-century Přemyslid fortress is still visible. On the edge of the cliffs above the river, however, you can see the remnants of the defensive bastion known as the Bath of Libuše. It's a spot where visitors can really sense the wild early days of Bohemia's ascendancy.

V pevnosti 5b, Prague 2 • www.praha-vysehrad.cz • 241 410 348 • Metro: Vyšehrad • Tram: 3, 7, 8, 16, 17, 24

Legionnaire's Bridge

5 A bronze relief on Legionnaire's Bridge (Most Legií) honors the Czech and Slovak soldiers who switched sides to fight against Germany and the Austro-Hungarian Empire in Russia during World War I (see sidebar right). After independence in 1918, Praguers embraced the bridge, which had originally been built in 1901 and named Franz I Bridge, as an icon of the new Czech and Slovak sovereignty.

Between Národní and Újezd, Prague 1 • Metro: Národní třída • Tram: 6, 9, 22

IN THE KNOW

The Czechoslovak Legion was formed out of a resistance movement established by Tomáš Garrigue Masaryk, leader of the Czechoslovak independence movement (and first president of Czechoslovakia in 1918) and Edvard Beneš. Its ranks were swelled by Czech and Slovak soldiers from the German and Austrian armies. In 1917, when Lenin took power and negotiated peace with Germany, the Czech units who had been fighting in Russia found themselves cut off and embroiled in the Soviet revolution. They escaped through Siberia, fighting groups of Bolsheviks along the way. On their return to Prague, they received an enthusiastic welcome.

Prague Castle

6 Bohemia's rise to power dates from the establishment of a bishopric at Prague Castle (Pražský hrad) in the 10th century. In the 14th century, Holy Roman Emperor Charles IV named Prague his capital. Two centuries later, Habsburg emperors Ferdinand II and Rudolf II also based their courts here. The full story of this ancient site is recounted in the Story of Prague Castle exhibition (see p. 120).

Hradčanské náměstí, Prague 1 • www.hrad.cz • 224 373 584 • Closed Dec. 24 • Metro: Staroměstská • Tram: 22

Prague for Art Nouveau & Cubism

Immerse yourself in the decorative forms of early 20th-century Czech art and design, before seeking out the city's unique modern architectural style.

5 **Vyšehrad Houses** (see p. 37) Architect Josef Chochol gave a group of six houses the cubist treatment, full of playful geometric shapes and corners.

4 **Jungmann's Square Lamppost** (see p. 37) The lamppost in this quiet square is an icon of Czech cubism. Walk south on Jungmannova to Charles Square (Karlovo náměstí). Walk east on Resslova and turn south on Rašínovo nábřeží.

Rudolfinu
Staromēsts
Klementinum
Betlémská kaple
Národr
MOST   divadlo
LEGII
JIRÁSKŮV
MOST   Karlo
Tančící dům   námé
NOVI
MĚSTI
Karlovo   RAŠÍNOVO NÁBŘEŽÍ
SMÍCHOV náměstí
• Anděl
VLTAVSKÁ   Vltava
Vyšehrad
Houses
5
0   500 meters
0   500 yards
Bazilika sv. Petra a
Pavla & Slavír
Smíchovské
nádraží

PRAGUE FOR ART NOUVEAU & CUBISM   DISTANCE: 3.1 MILES (5 KM)
TIME: 7 HOURS   METRO START: NÁMĚSTÍ REPUBLIKY

WHIRLWIND TOURS

❶ Municipal House (see pp. 36, 59–60)
The inner salons of this temple to art nouveau style present a rich array of frescoes, furnishings, light fittings, and an entire Mucha-inspired room. Walk along Hybernská and turn right onto Wilsonova.

DVOŘÁKOVO NÁBŘEŽÍ

Anežský klášter

Židovské muzeum

KE ŠTVANICI

Florenc

Kostel sv. Jakuba

❶ Municipal House
(Obecní dům)

Stavovské
divadlo

ucha Museum
chovo muzeum) **❸**

odní
Můstek
Hlavní
nádraží

❷ Main Railway Station
(Hlavní nádraží)

❹ Jungmann's Square Lamppost
(Jungmannovo náměstí)

Muzeum
ITALSKÁ
RIEGROVY
SADY

Národní
muzeum

Karlovo
náměstí

NÁMĚSTÍ
MÍRU

JEČNA
I.P. Pavlova

ÁTSKÁ
SOKOLSKÁ
LEGEROVA
NUSELSKÝ MOST

PI
NA SLUPI

SEKANINOVA

JAROMÍROVA

ŠEHRAD   ČIKLOVA
Vyšehrad

Rotunda
sv. Martina

❷ Main Railway Station (see p. 36) Admire the station's beautifully decorated dome, which crowns the busy concourse and platforms below. Take the lift or escalators down to the concourse level and leave by the Washingtonova exit. Walk along Růžová, turn left onto Jindřišská, and then right on Panská.

MUCHA   MUSEUM

❸ Mucha Museum (see pp. 37, 169) Housed in the baroque Kaunický Palace, the museum celebrates the life and work of the supreme master of art nouveau. Head west on Na Příkopě and turn left onto Jungmannovo Square (Jungmannovo náměstí).

WHIRLWIND TOURS

Municipal House

1 Visit this gorgeous casket of art nouveau style and content on a prebooked, hour-long tour of its smaller rooms and spaces (see website for dates and times). Original features in Municipal House (Obecní dům) include mirror walls and light fittings in the former **Confectionery,** wall panels, chandeliers, and marble tables in the **Moravian–Slovak Parlor,** and stenciling and stuccowork in the **Oriental Parlor.** The circular **Mayor's Hall** is suffused with Alphons Mucha's splendid decoration. Light filters through his blue doves-and-flowers stained-glass window, and his ceiling fresco "Slavic Concorde" and surrounding murals celebrate Czech heroism and the desire for Slavic unity.

Náměstí Republiky 5, Prague 1 • www.obecnidum.cz • 222 002 101 • Tour: $$ • Metro: Náměstí Republiky • Tram: 5, 8, 24, 26

A detail from Alphons Mucha's designs illustrating civic virtues in the Mayor's Hall at Municipal House

Main Railway Station

2 The first train arrived at Prague's main railway station (Hlavní nádraží) in December 1871, but architect Josef Fanta reconstructed the station between 1901 and 1909 in pure secession style. Step inside the upper level via Wilsonova to see the recently restored, golden dome emblazoned with coats of arms. Tucked underneath, the **Fantova kavárna,** also restored, allows you to sip a coffee while absorbing the surrounding beauties of statuary, stained-glass windows, and the flamboyant, original station entrance proclaimed by cunningly draped nude figures over a leafy arch.

Wilsonova 8, Prague 2 • http://czech-transport.com • 221 111 122 • Metro: Hlavní nádraží • Tram: 5, 9, 26

Mucha Museum

3 This small museum (Muchovo muzeum) dedicated to Alphons Mucha, one of the most celebrated exponents of sensuous art nouveau, includes posters, paintings, drawings, and photographs. There are countless examples of his classically beautiful Slavic maidens with rippling hair in curvilinear floral settings. Also look out for quirkier exhibits, such as a photograph taken in his Paris studio of the painter Paul Gauguin—sans culottes—on the harmonium.

Panská 7, Prague 1 • www.mucha.cz • 224 216 415 • $$ • Closed Jan. 1, Dec. 24–25 • Metro: Můstek • Tram: 3, 9

Jungmann's Square Lamppost

4 This tall, faceted concrete lamppost in a corner of Jungmannovo náměstí (square) is a must-see for lovers of cubist architecture. Designed by Emil Králíček, it is the only cubist-style lamppost in the world.

Jungmannovo náměstí, Prague 1 • Metro: Můstek • Tram: 3, 17

Vyšehrad Houses

5 Angles, chunky shapes, and terra-cotta or putty colors exemplify this group of six cubist-style houses built in the early 20th century at the foot of the Vyšehrad promontory. The row of three houses at **Rasínovo nábřeží 6–10** have a faceted mansard roof and gables. The **Villa Kovarovic** (Kovařovicova vila), round the corner on Libušina (No. 3), has a cubist garden, even including the metal fence and steps. Walk to the end of Libušina and turn right onto Neklanova. The facades of apartment buildings at **Neklanova 30** and **Neklanova 2** consist of faceted and fluted pyramid shapes that create constantly changing patterns of light and shadow. All six are the work of Josef Chochol, who translated the fractured planes and forms of cubist art into building design to create a specifically Czech architectural style.

Rašínovo nábřeží, Prague 2 • Metro: Karlovo náměstí • Tram: 3, 17

Prague in a Weekend with Kids

Malayan tigers, marionettes, and an ancient castle are all part of the adventure on day one of your family weekend in Prague.

Prague Zoo **1**

5 Prague Castle (see pp. 41, 118–124)
Royal treasure, colorful stained-glass windows, medieval armor and weapons, and a toy museum are among the many attractions for kids.

4 Kampa Island (see pp. 41, 102) Explore the island's riverside park, playground, and giant sculptures. Go west on Harantova and turn north onto Karmelitská. Follow Nerudova west and turn onto Ke Hradu. Or take tram 22 from Karmelitská to the Poholeřec stop.

PODBABSKÁ
PAPÍRENSKÁ
ZELENÁ
JUGOSLÁVSKÝCH PARTYZÁNŮ
TERRONSKÁ
ANTONÍNA ČERMÁKA
ROOSEVELTOVA
WOLKER
BUBENEČSKÁ
Dejvická
BUBENEČ
ČESKOSLOVENSKÉ ARMÁDY
POD KAŠT
SVATOVÍTSKÁ
Hradčanská
BALB
PEVNOSTNÍ
JELENÍ

Prague Castle **5**
(Pražský hrad)
Malostransk
Truhlář Marionettes
(Marionety Truhlář)
3

Kostel Panny Marie Vítězné
Kampa Island 4

KINSKY GARDENS
VÍTĚZNÁ

WHIRLWIND TOURS

**WEEKEND WITH KIDS DAY 1   DISTANCE: 6.3 MILES (10.2 KM)
TIME: 7 HOURS   METRO START: NÁDRAŽÍ HOLEŠOVICE**

❶ Prague Zoo (see p. 40) Romp through an Indonesian rain forest or go neck to neck with giraffes roaming a re-creation of the African savanna at one of Europe's largest, most progressive zoos. Take bus 112 (or the Zoobus April–Sept.) to Nádraží Holešovice Metro stop, and then take tram 5, 12, 14, 15, or 17 to the Exhibition Grounds.

❷ Exhibition Grounds (see pp. 40–41, 159–160) The city's historic fairgrounds host an amusement park and an aquarium. Take tram 12 to the northern end of U Lužického semináře and walk south.

❸ Truhlář Marlonettes (see pp. 41, 90–91) Purchase one of Truhlář's handmade string puppets or sign up for marionette-making workshops at their Staré Město factory. At the southern end of U Lužického semináře, cross the pedestrian bridge and follow cobblestoned Na Kampě beneath Charles Bridge.

This ten-day-old Komodo dragon is part of Prague Zoo's breeding program for endangered species.

Prague Zoo

① Set on a bend in the Vltava River downstream from the city center, Prague Zoo sprawls across a vast expanse of woodland and meadows. Displays take you up close and personal with the animals, many of which are housed in large enclosures that replicate their natural habitats as far as possible. The zoo has a busy conservation program and is strong on endangered creatures like the Galápagos tortoise, Chinese giant salamander, gharial crocodile, and Przewalski's horse.

U Trojského zámku 120, Prague 7 • www.zoopraha.cz/en • 296 112 230 • $$
• Metro: Nádraží Holešovice, then bus 112 (or Zoobus April–Sept.) • Riverboat
(daily May–Aug., weekends April and Sept.): Císařský ostrov

Exhibition Grounds

② A roller coaster, Ferris wheel, and bumper cars operate at the **amusement park** in the Exhibition Grounds (Výstaviště) in Holešovice. Each March, during the annual St. Matthew Fair

(Matějská pout'; *$, closed Mon.*), the regular funfair expands to more than 100 rides and attractions. The **Sea World** aquarium (Mořský svět: *www.morsky-svet.cz, $$*) will appeal to fish fans.

Areál Výstaviště 67, Prague 7 • www.incheba.cz • 220 103 111 • Metro: Nádraží Holešovice • Tram: 5, 12, 14, 15, 17

Truhlář Marionettes

3 The Truhlář marionette factory (Marionety Truhlář) makes all sorts of stringed wooden puppets, from classics like jesters and skeletons to robots and Wild West gunslingers. Truhlář also offers marionette-making sessions at its workshops in Staré Město (*$$$$$*).

U Lužického semináře 5, Prague 1 • www.marionety.com • 602 689 918 • Metro: Malostranská

Kampa Island

4 This slice of old Prague is separated from Malá Strana by an old mill run called the Devil's Stream (Čertovka). Kids can let off steam in the Čertovka playground or play Frisbee in the park. Walk through the grounds of the Kampa Museum (see p. 167) to see statues of a red horse and rider and two giant babies.

U Sovových mlýnů 2, Prague 1 • www.museumkampa.com • 257 286 147 • $ • Metro: Malostranská • Tram: 20, 22

Prague Castle

5 Catch the Changing of the Guard ceremony on the hour at the front gate. The Story of Prague Castle exhibition (see p. 120) includes a game for children in which they choose a role connected with the castle's history and complete tasks and missions to find out about that person.

Hradčanské náměstí, Prague 1 • 224 373 368 • www.hrad.cz • Closed Dec. 24 • Metro: Malostranská • Tram: 22

SAVVY **TRAVELER**

In summer, the coolest way to travel to and from the zoo is by the Prague Steamboat Company's 75-minute cruise along the Vltava River (*www.prague steamboats.com, 224 931 013, $ one way, daily May–Aug., weekends April and Sept.*). You get great views of the city skyline en route. Boats run between Rašinovo Quay in Nové Město and Emperor's Island (Císařský Ostrov) near the zoo with a stop at Čech Bridge (Čechův most).

Prague in a Weekend with Kids

Peer down on old Prague from three different viewpoints on an outing that also includes paddleboats and a magical clock.

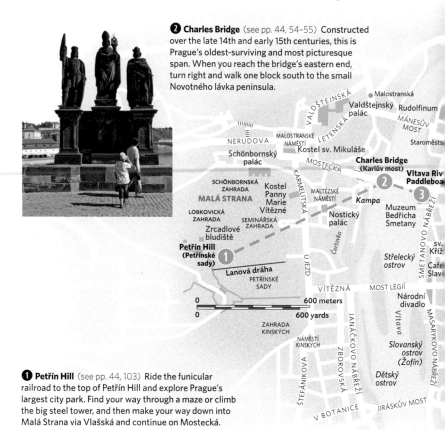

2 Charles Bridge (see pp. 44, 54–55) Constructed over the late 14th and early 15th centuries, this is Prague's oldest-surviving and most picturesque span. When you reach the bridge's eastern end, turn right and walk one block south to the small Novotného lávka peninsula.

VALDŠTEJNSKÁ

LETENSKÁ

Malostranská

Valdštejnský palác · Rudolfinum

MÁNESŮV MOST

NERUDOVA · MALOSTRANSKÉ NÁMĚSTÍ

Schönbornský palác · Kostel sv. Mikuláše · Staroměsts

MOSTECKÁ

KARMELITSKÁ

Charles Bridge (Karlův most) · **Vltava Riv Paddleboa**

SCHÖNBORNSKÁ ZAHRADA · Kostel Panny Marie Vítězné

MALÉ STRANA

LOBKOVICKÁ ZAHRADA

SEMINÁŘSKÁ ZAHRADA

Zrcadlové bludiště

MALTÉZSKÉ NÁMĚSTÍ · Kampa

Nostický palác

Muzeum Bedřicha Smetany

SMETANOVO NÁBŘEŽÍ

sv. Kříž

Petřín Hill (Petřínské sady) **1**

Lanová dráha

PETŘÍNSKÉ SADY

Čertovka

Střelecký ostrov · Café Slav

ÚJEZD

VÍTĚZNÁ · MOST LEGIÍ

Národní divadlo

Vltava

0 ——— 600 meters
0 ——— 600 yards

ZAHRADA KINSKÝCH

NÁMĚSTÍ KINSKÝCH

JANÁČKOVO NÁBŘEŽÍ

ZBOROVSKÁ

MASARYKOVO NÁBŘEŽÍ

Slovanský ostrov (Žofín)

Dětský ostrov

ŠTEFÁNIKOVA

V BOTANICE · JIRÁSKŮV MOST

1 Petřín Hill (see pp. 44, 103) Ride the funicular railroad to the top of Petřín Hill and explore Prague's largest city park. Find your way through a maze or climb the big steel tower, and then make your way down into Malá Strana via Vlašská and continue on Mostecká.

**WEEKEND WITH KIDS DAY 2   DISTANCE: 2.2 MILES (3.5 KM)
TIME: 6-7 HOURS   METRO START: MALOSTRANSKÁ**

WHIRLWIND TOURS

⑤ Kotva Roof Terrace (see pp. 45, 152) The roof of Kotva department store offers yet another spectacular view of Prague, as well as a playground and alfresco café.

④ Old Town Square (see pp. 45, 62–65) Watch the Astronomical Clock and climb the Old Town Hall Tower to look down on old Prague. Leave the square on Celetná. At Náměstí Republiky, turn left and walk to the northern end of the square.

Central Prague
Area enlarged above

③ Vltava River Paddleboats (see p. 45) Rent a paddleboat and spend an hour on the river admiring Prague's medieval skyline. Follow the riverside road one block north and turn east onto Karlova.

WHIRLWIND TOURS

Petřín Hill

1 Ride the funicular railroad from medieval Malá Strana to the summit of Petřín Hill (Petřín) and then hike across the top of Prague's inner-city highlands. If the view still isn't high enough, scamper to the top of the Observation Tower (Petřínská rozhledna), a miniature Eiffel Tower. The park also offers pony rides, an observatory, and a mirror maze.

Karmelitská, Prague 1 • www.dpp.cz/en/the-petrin-funicular • 296 191 817 • $
• Metro: Malostranská • Tram: 20, 22

Charles Bridge

2 Leaping the Vltava River on 16 arches, Charles Bridge (Karlův most) is one of the world's most spectacular bridges. The bridge is renowned for its Gothic towers at either end and the 30 saintly statues ranged along its balustrades. Kids enjoy touching the relief image of St. John of Nepomuk below his statue and making a wish.

Křižovnické náměstí, Prague 1 • Metro: Malostranská, Můstek • Tram: 17, 18

See several versions of yourself in the Petřín Hill mirror maze.

Vltava River Paddleboats

3 Take to the river in one of the rubber-duck-yellow paddleboats rented by the hour at Novotného lávka. Because of the weir, you'll have to paddle downriver from here, but there's plenty to see on both shores and Prague Castle looms in the distance.

Novotného lávka 201/1, Prague 1 · www.lavka.cz · 221 082 299 · $$ per hour · Closed Nov.–April · Metro: Karlovo náměstí · Tram: 14, 17

Old Town Square

4 The heart of Prague for 1,000 years, this large cobblestone plaza (Staroměstské náměstí) buzzes with people night and day. Look out for the street performers, who can include buskers, fire-spinners, and living statues. Or have a go at popping giant bubbles. Be there at the top of the hour to see Death ring a bell to summon a parade of 12 saints across the Astronomical Clock (Orloj) on the front of the Old Town Hall (Staroměstská radnice). Then climb the town hall tower (or take the elevator) for a bird's-eye view of the city.

Staroměstské náměstí, Prague 1 · www.staromestskaradnicepraha.cz · 236 002 629 · Tower: $ · Metro: Staroměstská · Tram: 17, 18

Kotva Roof Terrace

5 Another great view awaits on the roof terrace atop Kotva department store. This alfresco area boasts a café with a small playground, coloring books, Lego bricks, and a family-friendly menu. It's especially nice around sunset with the silhouetted spires and steeples of old Prague all around.

Revoluční 1/655 · www.od-kotva.cz, Prague 1 · 224 801 111 · Metro: Náměstí Republiky

GOOD **EATS**

■ **U KRÁLE BRABANTSKÉHO**
Let your kids get medieval at this theme restaurant near Prague Castle in Hradčany. The menu runs heavy on roasted meats and vegetables, but the real attraction is the medieval entertainment—swordsmen, fire-eaters, drummers, and belly dancers in a candlelit, catacomb-like atmosphere. **Thunovská 198/15, 602 524 725, $**

■ **VYTOPNA RAILWAY RESTAURANT**
Miniature trains deliver the drinks to your table at this combination restaurant and model railway hall on Wenceslas Square in Nové Město. The extensive selection includes pasta, chicken, fish, and meat dishes, soups and salads, lovely desserts, and a special kids' menu. **Václavské náměstí 56, 725 190 646, $$$**

PART 2

Prague's Neighborhoods

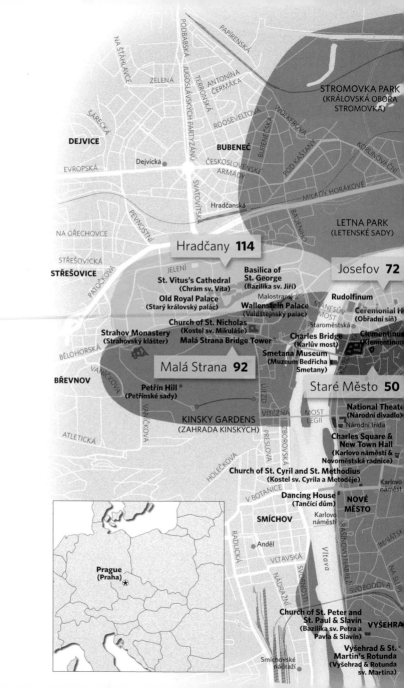

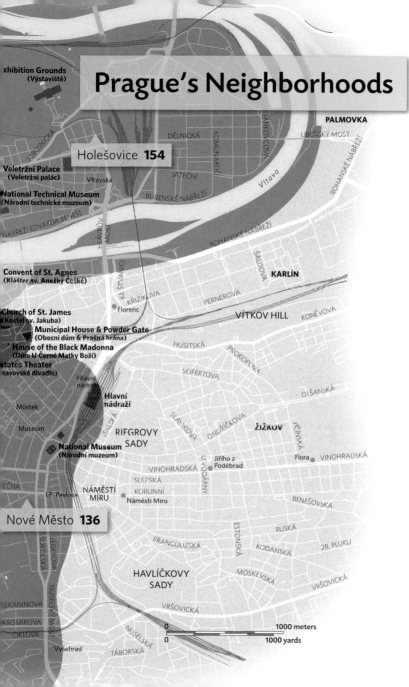

Prague's Neighborhoods

xhibition Grounds
(Výstaviště)

PALMOVKA

DĚLNICKÁ

LIBEŇSKÝ MOST

Holešovice 154

STROJNICKÁ

Veletržní Palace
(Veletržní palác)

Vltavská

JATEČNÍ

Vltava

ROHANSKÉ NÁBŘEŽÍ

National Technical Museum
(Národní technické muzeum)

BUBENSKÉ NÁBŘEŽÍ

NÁBŘEŽÍ EDVARDA BENEŠE

HLÁVKŮV MOST

ROHANSKÉ NÁBŘEŽÍ

ŠALDOVA

KARLÍN

Convent of St. Agnes
(Klášter sv. Anežky České)

KE ŠTVANICI

KŘIŽÍKOVA

PERNEROVA

Florenc

Church of St. James
(Kostel sv. Jakuba)

VÍTKOV HILL

KONĚVOVA

Municipal House & Powder Gate
(Obecní dům & Prašná brána)

HUSITSKÁ

PROKOPOVA

House of the Black Madonna
(Dům U Černé Matky Boží)

states Theater
tavovské divadlo)

Hlavní
nádraží

SEIFERTOVA

OLŠANSKÁ

**Hlavní
nádraží**

Můstek

TRIAŽCÍ

SLAVÍKOVA

ONDŘÍČKOVA

ŽIŽKOV

AČINSKÁ

Muzeum

**RIFGROVY
SADY**

National Museum
(Národní muzeum)

Flora

VINOHRADSKÁ

Jiřího z
Poděbrad

VINOHRADSKÁ

VINOHRADSKÁ

SLEZSKÁ

EČNA

I.P. Pavlova

**NÁMĚSTÍ
MÍRU**

KORUNNÍ

U VODÁRNY

Náměstí Míru

BENEŠOVSKÁ

LEGEROVA

Nové Město 136

SOKOLSKÁ

RUSKÁ

FRANCOUZSKÁ

ESTONSKÁ

KODAŇSKÁ

28. PLUKU

**HAVLÍČKOVY
SADY**

MOSKEVSKÁ

VRŠOVICKÁ

NUSELSKÝ MOST

SEKANINOVA

AROMÍROVA

VRŠOVICKÁ

CIKLOVA

NUSELSKÁ

0   1000 meters

0   1000 yards

Vyšehrad

TÁBORSKÁ

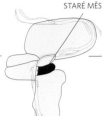

Staré Město

Redolent with history you can walk through, pass under, and explore, the medieval heart of Prague is a world apart from modern Europe—and even from the rest of the Czech capital. Supported by flourishing trade and a king's charter, Staré Město (Old Town) started as a fortress town bounded on the north and west by the Vltava River and on the east and south by walls along the routes of the modern-day streets: Revoluční, Na Příkopě (At the Moat), and Národní.

Once the most important marketplace in the city, Old Town Square (Staroměstské náměstí) is still the hub of the tangle of cobblestone streets, darkened Gothic spires, and countless passages that make up the area. Ornate doorways lead to shortcuts through narrow, stone-walled spaces, deep cellars, and interior courtyards. The medieval street layout rewards walkers with stops at fabulously intricate churches and palaces and characterful galleries, cafés, and shops.

○ Romantic Staré Město beckons to walkers as they approach across the Charles Bridge.

Staré Město

Old Town remains a living time capsule with palaces, chapels, and cellar pubs all jammed into a joyous jumble of medieval streets.

⑤ Clam-Gallas Palace (see p. 57) Despite being up a side street, the opulent facade of this baroque palace is easy to spot. Continue east on Karlova.

① Charles Bridge (see pp. 54–55) Enter Staré Město as Emperor Charles IV did, strolling across the 14th-century bridge named for him. Turn right onto Smetanovo nábřeží.

② Smetana Museum (see p. 55) Look around this shrine dedicated to composer Bedřich Smetana and enjoy the views across the river. Head along Anenská and turn right onto Liliová.

③ Bethlehem Chapel (see p. 56) Look out for the stark lines of this large 14th-century chapel towering above its medieval neighbors. Walk back up Liliová to Karlova.

④ Clementinum (see pp. 56–57) Stroll through the courtyards of this former Jesuit College. Walk east on Karlova and turn left onto Husova.

STARÉ MĚSTO   DISTANCE: 2 MILES (3.2 KM)
TIME: APPROX. 6 HOURS   METRO START: STAROMĚSTSKÁ

6 Old Town Square (see pp. 62–65) Soak up the atmosphere in this large square packed with historic sights. Walk one block east.

7 Church of St. James (see pp. 58–59) Admire the ornate interior of this baroque sanctuary. Walk south on Rybná and turn left onto Celetná.

MASNÁ

Church of St. James (Kostel sv. Jakuba)

RYBNÁ

7

Old Town Square (Staroměstské náměstí)

6

Municipal House & Powder Gate (Obecní dům & Prašná brána)

8

House of the Black Madonna (Dům U Černé Matky Boží)

9

CELETNÁ

MALÉ NÁMĚSTÍ

MELANTRICHOVA

ŽELEZNÁ

OVOCNÝ TRH

10 Estates Theater (Stavovské divadlo)

RYTÍŘSKÁ

HAVELSKÁ

Můstek

10 Estates Theater (see p. 61) Imagine this elegant baroque theater in the days of Wolfgang Amadeus Mozart. Walk southwest on Rytířská and continue on Skořepka.

8 Municipal House & Powder Gate (see pp. 59–60) Marvel at some of Prague's most extravagant art nouveau decoration at the Municipal House. The building is connected to a medieval tower that was part of the Old Town wall. Walk one block west on Celetná.

9 House of the Black Madonna (see p. 60) Enjoy the finest example of cubist architecture and interior design in Bohemia. Stroll southwest along Ovocný trh.

STARÉ MĚSTO

An image of St. John of Nepomuk on the Charles Bridge gleams from the touch of luck-seekers.

Charles Bridge

1 Designed by architect Peter Parler on the orders of Emperor Charles IV, the 16-arch Charles Bridge (Karlův most) has spanned the Vltava River since its completion in 1402. Built using granite blocks held together with mortar made from eggs, it has proven remarkably solid, broken only by a succession of floods in 1890. Most of the statues of saints standing watch on the bridge are 19th-century copies of original masterworks by such sculptors as Matthias Braun and Jan Brokoff that were added during the Counter Reformation as propaganda for the Catholic Habsburg rulers of Bohemia. One of the few originals is that of **St. John of Nepomuk** (see sidebar opposite), eight places in from the Malá Strana embankment on the downstream side and recognizable from the saint's five-starred halo. Thousands of visitors have touched a bronze plaque at the spot illustrating St. John's martyrdom in the hope that this will ensure their return to Prague one day. The **Old Town Bridge Tower** has good views from the top, and the **Charles Bridge Museum** (Muzeum Karlova mostu; *Křižovnické náměstí, www.muzeumkarlovamostu.cz, $*) illustrates the construction efforts and ingenious solutions of 14th-century builders.

Křižovnické náměstí, Prague 1 • Metro: Staroměstská • Tram: 17, 18

IN THE **KNOW**

John of Nepomuk, one of the Czech Republic's national saints, was confessor to the wife of King Wenceslas IV. Legend has it that the king ordered the priest to be thrown from the Charles Bridge because he refused to reveal the queen's confessions, and that a group of stars appeared at the spot where he drowned.

Smetana Museum

2 This small museum (Muzeum Bedřicha Smetany) close to the Charles Bridge was established in 1936 to celebrate the life and work of one of Bohemia's most admired composers. Bedřich Smetana penned operas and symphonic poems, including the tone poem *Má vlast*, or *My Country*—Czechs regard a section dedicated to the confluence of the Vltava and Labe Rivers as a second national anthem. Exhibits include manuscripts, set and costume designs, and photographs relating to Smetana's life and work, but the building alone is worth the price of admission. Formerly the Old Town waterworks, this stunning neo-Renaissance structure built in 1883–1884 enjoys the finest riverfront views of any building in the city, surrounded as it is on three sides by the babbling Vltava— a fitting location for a memorial to the 19th-century composer and his mellifluous works.

Novotného lávka 1, Prague 1 • www.nm.cz • 222 220 082 • $ • Closed Tues. • Metro: Staroměstská • Tram: 17, 18

One of the Smetana Museum's original costume designs for Smetana's opera *The Bartered Bride*

STARÉ MĚSTO

IN **THE KNOW**

Some of Old Town's most striking statues from the baroque era are the work of sculptor Matthias Braun. Born in Switzerland in 1684, Braun trained in Vienna and Italy before settling in Prague after 1710. His figures, which come alive through flowing lines and gestures, appear to wrestle with their feelings in true baroque style. You can see examples of his work at the **Clam-Gallas Palace** (see opposite) and in the **Church of St. Clement** (*Karlova 1*), which houses some 170 of his woodcarvings and statues. The statues of St. Ivo, St. Ludmilla, and St. Luthgard on the **Charles Bridge** (see pp. 54–55) are also by him. In his later years Braun developed tuberculosis and by the time he died in 1738, his nephew Antonín Braun had taken over his workshop.

STARÉ MĚSTO

Bethlehem Chapel

3 Built in 1391, the Bethlehem Chapel (Betlémská kaple) was the result of a political compromise that allowed the Czech proto-Protestant movement founded and led by Jan Hus (see sidebar p. 64) to flourish in Prague. The Catholic authorities would not permit the reformers to build a church, thus this surprisingly modern-looking house of worship was officially deemed a chapel. Nevertheless, its dimensions are on a par with most other churches in Staré Město, and it seats 3,000 people. From the beginning, the chapel was a hotbed of revolution, with services conducted in Czech rather than the German-language Masses usually offered to Bohemia's faithful. Jan Hus led the congregation here from 1402 until he fell foul of the authorities in 1412. Masses and concerts are well worth a visit.

Betlémské náměstí 4, Prague 1 • www.suz.cvut.cz • 224 248 595 • Metro: Můstek • Tram: 6, 9, 18, 22

Clementinum

4 The Jesuit Order founded this large complex of churches and historic buildings in 1556. By the time Hapsburg Empress Maria Theresa expelled the Order from Bohemia in the mid-18th century, it had established a university, library, and observatory on the site. Today, the Clementinum houses the Czech Republic's National Library. Entrances on Křižovnická and Karlova lead to a series of quiet inner courtyards, but if you want to see the richly decorated baroque interiors, you need to take a guided tour from the visitors' entrance on Karlova. On the ground floor, the **Mirror**

Chapel (1724) has frescoes by Jan Hiebl and intricate stuccowork inset with mirror panels on the ceiling. Chamber concerts are held daily in this richly adorned space. Upstairs, the **Baroque Library** (1722) has a trompe l'oeil ceiling painted by Jan Hiebl and walls lined with leather-bound books. Devices in the floor and roof of the Clementinum's south and east annexes have recorded the temperature three times a day since 1752, making it one of the oldest meteorological stations in Central Europe.

Mariánské náměstí 5, Prague 1 • www.klementinum.com • 222 220 879 • $$ • Metro: Můstek, Staroměstská • Tram: 17, 18

Clam-Gallas Palace

5 In a city full of extravagant 18th-century architecture, the stately Clam-Gallas Palace (Clam-Gallasův palác) carries the standard with its classic late baroque design dating from 1713. Look for the monumental sculptures by Matthias Braun on the front facade. The former palace now houses the city archives, and for most of the year only the exterior is visible to the public, but annual concert series in February and August allow you to glide up the main staircase with its sculptures by Braun and ceiling fresco by Italian artist Carlo Carlone, view the upstairs rooms with their intricate stuccowork and frescoes, and catch sight of the Vltava fountain by Václav Prachner set into the garden wall.

Husova 20, Prague 1 • www.pragueexperience .com • 236 001 111 • Metro: Staroměstská • Tram: 17, 18

Monumental sculptures flank the entrance to the Clam-Gallas Palace.

STARÉ MĚSTO

Old Town Square

6 See pp. 62–65.

Between Maiselova, U Radnice, and Celetná • www.praguewelcome.cz • Metro: Staroměstská • Tram: 17, 18

Church of St. James

7 The soaring ceilings of this hard-to-miss church, the largest in Prague after St. Vitus's Cathedral, provide outstanding acoustics for the thundering organ recitals and other concerts that take place here after Sunday Mass and on some weekday evenings. But most visitors to the Church of St. James (Kostel sv. Jakuba) are attracted by the twin appeal of the epic carving of the Fall on the church's front facade, an 18th-century addition, and the **mummified object**—said to be a human arm—hanging just inside the entrance. According to legend, the arm once belonged to a

The Municipal House's French restaurant serves contemporary food in an original art nouveau setting.

thief who tried to steal the jewels on a likeness of the Virgin Mary within. The story goes that she promptly grabbed his wrist and refused to let go, making amputation his only means of escape. The "arm" was left on display as an object lesson to anyone else who might be contemplating criminal activity. Probably more inspiring are the 20 or more side chapels, particularly the floridly ornate **tomb of Count Jan Vratislav of Mitrovice,** an influential Bohemian lord chancellor buried here in the 1700s.

Malá Štupartská 6, Prague 1 • http://minorite.cz • 224 828 814 • Metro: Náměstí Republiky • Tram: 5, 8, 24, 26

Municipal House & Powder Gate

8 The mundane name would not lead you to guess at the splendor of this gem of art nouveau style built from 1906 to 1912, but Municipal House (Obecní dům) features a classic Mitteleuropa coffeehouse with high ceilings and precious little cakes; a top-floor gallery for temporary exhibitions with Bohemian connections, such as part of the Czech and European art nouveau collection from the Museum of Decorative Arts; and the vast **Smetana Hall,** home to the Prague Symphony Orchestra. This historic hall witnessed the signing into existence of the sovereign state of Czechoslovakia on October 28, 1918.

Guided tours of the building's halls and conference rooms are available on days when they are not rented out for business functions (tour dates and times are announced a month in advance on the website). Concerts take place in the Smetana Hall every evening and the celebrated annual classical music festival, Prague Spring (*www.festival.cz*), kicks off here each May. The hall's stunning mosaic ceilings illustrating mythic scenes

GOOD **EATS**

■ **COTTO CRUDO**
Prague's first Michelin-star winner, located in the Four Seasons Hotel, has great views of Prague Castle to go with its Tuscan menu and excellent wine list. **Veleslavínova 2a, Prague 1, 221 426 880, $$$$$**

■ **LEHKÁ HLAVA**
With a name meaning Clear Head, this vegetarian spot is a sanctuary for lovers of healthy, light dishes based on seasonal ingredients. **Boršov 2, Prague 1, 222 220 665, $$**

■ **U MODRÉ KACHNIČKY**
The Blue Duckling's cozy dining room features traditional game-based Bohemian fare, such as roast duck in wild berry sauce with dumplings. **Michalská 16, Prague 1, 224 213 418, $$$**

STARÉ MĚSTO

from the Czech founding legends and memorials to the Czech Legionnaires of World War I are surpassed only by the paintings of Alphons Mucha in the Mayor's Hall.

The adjoining **Powder Gate** (Prašná brána), with its detailed Gothic tracing, is a last surviving remnant of the fortifications that once surrounded Staré Město. The present tower dates from 1475 and was built by King Vratislav II before he chose to escape his angry subjects by moving to Prague Castle. The tower was subsequently used as a store for gunpowder.

Náměstí Republiky 5, Prague 1 • www.obecnidum.cz • 222 002 101 • Concerts: $-$$$$$; Tour: $$ • Metro: Náměstí Republiky • Tram: 5, 8, 24, 26

A vase typical of the cubist ceramics on sale in the Kubista gallery

House of the Black Madonna

9 With its bold, multifaceted facade, the House of the Black Madonna (Dům U Černé Matky Boží) is the city's quintessential example of the Czech flair for cubist architecture. It was the creation of designer Josef Gočár, a leading figure in the Prague modernist movement, and opened in 1911 as a department store. The building's name derives from a statue that decorated one of the baroque houses that originally stood on the site. The Madonna lives on now in a golden cage attached to the house's northeast corner. The building is probably best enjoyed from the **Grand Café Orient** (see p. 70), one of the finest cubist-style interiors anywhere in the world, reached by an elegantly looping spiral staircase with stark black-and-white balustrade. The **Kubista** gallery, a shop on the ground floor, sells reproduction cubist dinnerware and decorative items along with jewelry, glass, and printed scarves by contemporary Czech designers.

Ovocný trh 19, Prague 1 • www.kubista.cz • 224 236 378 • Metro: Náměstí Republiky • Tram: 5, 8, 24, 26

Estates Theater

10 A neoclassical wedding cake of a performance space designed by Anton Haffenecker for František Antonín Count Nostitz Rieneck in 1783, the Estates Theater (Stavovské divadlo) was chosen by Mozart for the world premier of his opera *Don Giovanni* in 1787. The multitiered, oval-shaped auditorium is so evocative of the period that director Miloš Forman made extensive use of it in his 1984 film *Amadeus*. It has subsequently hosted some of the world's greatest conductors, including Carl Maria von Weber and Gustav Mahler. Today, the theater (which is one of five in the city administered by the National Theater) puts on opera and ballet. The auditorium's powder-blue-hued decor and gilt-edged balcony boxes have been lovingly restored in recent years.

Ovocný trh 1, Prague 1 • www.estatestheatre.cz • 224 901 448 • Metro: Můstek • Tram: 6, 9, 18, 22

A scene from Miloš Forman's *Amadeus* in the Estates Theater

STARÉ MĚSTO

Old Town Square

*A public space at the heart of the city's oldest district, the square
bears traces of at least eight centuries of history.*

Cafés line the square in summer, offering a chance to relax.

This former market square is at the meeting point of all the main streets in
Staré Město. Its array of buildings feature many overlaid elements from the
city's past lives, from Gothic facades to World War II artillery scars. The
history of the Bohemian resistance to Habsburg rule, the city's bold embrace
of Renaissance-era technological wonders, and the spirit of Czech national
identity are also visible in the ornamental structures on and around the
square. Begin in the southwest corner as you approach from Karlova.

■ OLD TOWN HALL & ASTRONOMICAL CLOCK

Old Town Hall (Staroměstská radnice; *Staroměstské náměstí 1, 224 482 751, www.staromestskaradnicepraha.cz*) and its Astronomical Clock, or *Orloj,* jostle for No. 1 must-see status with Prague Castle and the Charles Bridge.

You can find the clock set into the blackened wall of the town hall's tower. Imperial clockmaker Mikuláš of Kadaň built it in 1410, and in 1490 clockmaster Hanuš Růže perfected its workings to create an engineering feat almost unrivaled at the time. Thanks to a series of intricate, interconnected gears and gauges, the clock shows Central European, Old Bohemian, and Babylonian time, the movements of the Sun and planets around the Earth, and a zodiacal wheel. Just before the clock strikes the hour, mechanical figures representing Death, the Turk, Vanity, and Greed spring into action and windows above the clock open to reveal a parade of apostles rolling by.

The town hall's main entrance gives access to the 228-foot-high (70 m) **tower** *($)*, built in 1338. Take the stairs or elevator to the top for one of the best views of the city (see p. 152). You can also visit the second-floor gallery, where **City**

see p. 152

Gallery Prague *(www.praha.cz, $)* holds temporary exhibitions, and take a guided tour *($)* of the **ceremonial halls** and **cellars.** In the latter, you can see the rooms of a simple 12th century home, including its drinking wells, as well as burned beams damaged during the Prague Uprising against the Nazi occupiers at the end of World War II. The Czech resistance movement had hidden a cache of weapons here, prompting a tank attack that destroyed the northern end of the town hall.

■ CHURCH OF OUR LADY BEFORE TÝN

On the square's east side is the imposing Church of Our Lady Before Týn (Kostel Matky Boží před Týnem; *Staroměstské náměstí, 222 318 186, closed Mon.*). It dates from 1385 and shows the influence of architects

STARÉ MĚSTO

IN **THE KNOW**

The religious reformer and martyr Jan Hus was born around 1370 and joined the priesthood in 1400. His opposition to the selling of indulgences and other abuses of church power and his attacks over the living conditions of the poor brought him into conflict with the church and secular authorities. The Pope excommunicated him in 1410, and in 1415 he was put on trial and burned at the stake.

Matthias of Arras—who also shaped St. Vitus's Cathedral—and Peter Parler. Inside, soaring vaulted ceilings, pink stucco walls festooned with rococo detail, fabulously ornate organ pipes built in 1673 by Heinrich Mundt, and a rich altarpiece painted by Karel Škréta wow visitors. Among the densely

A stone bell identifies the eponymous house, now an art gallery.

decorated tombs and chapels lie some of Czech history's most notable nobles. At the southern end, near the apse, look for the well-worn, dark marble slab that marks the **tomb of Tycho Brahe,** court astronomer to Emperor Rudolph II.

■ STONE BELL HOUSE

The austere, boxy structure next to the Týn Church is Stone Bell House (Dům U Kamenného zvonu; *Staroměstské náměstí 13, www.praha.eu, 224 828 245, $, closed Mon.*). Dating from the latter part of the 12th century, it features the oldest surviving Gothic facade in Prague, with arches, decorative tracing, and high, narrow windows. It is now one of the prime venues used by **City Gallery Prague;** temporary exhibitions focus on young artists and important movements in Czech art, such as surrealism.

■ KINSKÝ PALACE

Historians can't agree whether Anselmo Lurago or Kilian Ignatz Dientzenhofer created this opulent rococo pile next to the Stone Bell House, but its rich lines were conceived over a decade from 1755. The original exterior was damaged in firefights on the square at the end of World War II and has been largely replaced. The palace now houses the National

Gallery's permanent collection of **Art of Asia and the Ancient Mediterranean** (*Staroměstské náměstí 12, www.ngprague.cz, 224 810 758, $, closed Mon.*). It's better known as the former German grammar school where writer Franz Kafka studied as a child.

■ CHURCH OF ST. NICHOLAS

An ornate baroque confection on the square's north side, the church of St. Nicholas (Kostel svatého Mikuláše; *Staroměstské náměstí, 224 828 245*) is a great place to catch chamber concerts by some of the city's most talented classical musicians. Unlike its namesake across the river in Malá Strana (see pp. 99–100), this St. Nick has had its interior all but stripped bare through the city's history of foreign occupations.

■ JAN HUS STATUE

The haunting, verdigris-colored statue of Jan Hus surrounded by followers and bearing the inscription *Pravda vítězí* (Truth Prevails) dominates the middle of Old Town Square. It is a reminder of the central role this religious reformer and martyr played in the history of Bohemia (see sidebar opposite).

A late-19th century mural of St. Wenceslas adorns the Štorch House on Old Town Square.

STARÉ MĚSTO

Between Maiselova, U Radnice, and Celetná • www.praguewelcome.cz • Metro: Staroměstská • Tram: 17, 18

Musical Prague

A reputation for musical excellence has been drawing composers and musicians to the city since the Middle Ages. Today, classical offerings can be found in every corner, from the grand Rudolfinum to the art nouveau splendor of the Municipal House. In addition, thundering organs and soaring strings ring out daily in churches, palaces, and museums across the city.

The sign of the three fiddles marks the house of the violin-makers who repaired Beethoven's violin on one of his visits to Prague. Opposite: A piano in the National Museum's collection that Mozart is said to have played.

STARÉ MĚSTO

Early Days

Early Czech music was for the most part ecclesiastical. Trained and paid church singers began appearing in the mid-13th century, and after the founding of Charles University in the second half of the 14th century Bohemia was one of Europe's most important musical centers. In 1583, Emperor Rudolph II moved his capital from Vienna to Prague. His personal orchestra, which accompanied services at St. Vitus's Cathedral, was one of the largest in Europe, and the continent's cognoscenti considered the Rudolphine court ensemble an example of musical perfection.

Baroque Heyday

During the 17th and 18th centuries, Prague gained a reputation as the conservatory of Europe. Jan Dismas Zelenka (1679–1745), who was born in Prague but worked at the royal court at Dresden, was the era's best-known composer, often compared to Johannes Sebastian Bach. Early baroque music isn't easy to find on the programs of contemporary orchestras, but the Prague ensemble Collegium Marianum *(www.collegiummarianum.cz)* is keeping this style of music alive through its concerts in historic Prague buildings.

In January 1787, Prague's reputation as a musical center drew a visit from Wolfgang Amadeus Mozart. He conducted *The Marriage of Figaro* at the **Estates Theater** (Stavovské divadlo; see p. 61) and received an enthusiastic welcome from the city—so much so that he returned later in the year to conduct the world premiere of his new opera *Don Giovanni,* also at the Estates Theater, on October 29. Mozart made two more visits to Prague, and his death in 1791 produced an outpouring of grief among the city's residents. Around 4,000 people attended his memorial service, which was held in Malá Strana's **Church of St. Nicholas** (Kostel sv. Mikuláše; see pp. 99–100) and featured a Requiem Mass performed by more than 100 musicians.

Five years after Mozart's death, Ludwig van Beethoven arrived on his first visit, staying at the Inn at the Golden Unicorn, now No. 11, on Lázeňská in Malá Strana. Today, it is an apartment

building called **Beethoven Palace** and has a bronze plaque to the composer on the exterior. During his second visit to Prague, in 1798, Beethoven premiered his Piano Concerto No. 1 in C Major.

Czech National Revival

Fast forward to the 19th century, the time of the independence movement known as the Czech national revival. The Prague Conservatory, founded in 1808 and one of the oldest music schools in Europe, was a great supporter of emerging talent, and composers took inspiration from Czech folklore and history. In 1834, František Škroup wrote the song "Kde domov můj" ("Where Is My Home"), the first verse of which is the Czech Republic's national anthem.

String quartet performances are a regular feature at the Dvořák Museum.

The two biggest Czech music stars—Bedřich Smetana and Antonín Dvořák—emerged onto the world stage at this time. Czechs regard Smetana as the father of Czech music. The concert hall in **Municipal House** (see pp. 59–60) is named for him, and his symphonic cycle *Má vlast (My Homeland)* opens the annual Prague Spring Music Festival, an international celebration held annually in May featuring orchestral concerts, opera, and chamber music at venues all over the city *(www.festival.cz)*. Dvořák, who is probably the better known composer internationally, is celebrated at the **Dvořák Museum** *(Vila Amerika, Ke Karlovu 20, www.nm.cz, 224 923 363, closed Mon., $)*. The collection of

STARÉ MĚSTO

manuscripts, sheet music, period photographs, and correspondence includes the score of his Ninth, or *New World,* Symphony, a recording of which Neil Armstrong took on the *Apollo 11* mission to the Moon.

20th-Century Upheaval

The Nazi occupation during World War II was a difficult time for musicians, but the public took heart from performances of works by Smetana, Dvořák, and Mozart. After the war, much pent-up energy was released; the Academy of Performing Arts was established in 1945, and the Syndicate of Czech Composers in 1946. That year also saw the first Prague Spring Music Festival. During the first decades of communist rule, some creative freedom was allowed, but this was crushed following the Warsaw Pact invasion of August 1968.

Catching a Concert

Today, the city's three opera houses, five orchestras, and concert halls such as Municipal House's Smetana Hall and the Rudolfinum (see p. 76) host national and international companies and soloists. Many old churches and palaces also put on regular concerts. The ornate interior of Staré Město's **St. Giles Church** (Kostel sv. Jiljí) echoes to recitals of Bach, Vivaldi, and Mozart played on the original baroque organ built in 1737. The Prague Symphony Orchestra uses the deconsecrated **Church of St. Simon & St. Jude** (Kostel sv. Šimona a Judy) for chamber concerts. And at the **Spanish Synagogue** (Španělská synagoga) you can catch programs ranging from Czech music to Gershwin to Jewish melodies.

SMALL **VENUES**

Bethlehem Chapel Regular classical concerts. Betlémské náměstí 4 (see p. 56), www.suz.cvut.cz

Church of St. Giles Regular organ recitals. Husova, www .pragueticketoffice.com

Church of St. Nicholas Regular concerts. Old Town Square (see p. 65), www.concertsinprague.eu

Church of St. Simon & St. Jude Concerts a few times a month year-round. Dušní ulice, www.prague ticketoffice.com

Dvořák Museum Regular chamber concerts Ke Karlovu 20, www. pragueticket office.com

Clementinum Daily concerts of baroque music in the Mirror Chapel. Karlova 1 (see pp. 56–57), www.clemen tinumconcerts.com

Lobkowicz Palace Daily chamber concerts at midday. Jiřská 3 (see pp. 128–129), www.lobkowicz.cz

Basilica of St. George Classical and jazz concerts. Third Courtyard, Prague Castle (see pp. 122–123), www.pragueticketoffice.com

Spanish Synagogue Nightly concerts. Vězeňská 1 (see pp. 82–83), www.jewish museum.cz

Café Society

The 1920s may have been the golden age for Prague's cafés, but you can still enjoy the city's rich tradition of café life. Whether you prefer art nouveau touches at the Louvre or intellectual haunts such as the Slavia, *kavárnas,* or cafés, provide ideal surroundings in which to rest cobblestone-weary feet.

STARÉ MĚSTO

■ GRAND CAFÉ ORIENT

Located on the first floor of the House of the Black Madonna (see p. 60), the Grand Café Orient combines the best of cubist design with views of Staré Město. The ceiling lights, bar, and other furnishings are based on Josef Gočár's original designs for the building. In summer the narrow balcony is an excellent place for people-watching, and year-round you can enjoy an inventive selection of coffees and a slice of cake.

Ovocný trh 19, • www.grandcafeorient.cz • 224 224 240 • Metro: Náměstí Republiky

■ MONTMARTRE

You may struggle to find the Montmartre in Staré Město's maze of streets. And on entering, you may think you've wandered back in time as the café is more than 100 years old and some of its furnishings look as if they could be originals. Mismatched chairs and tables, armchairs rescued from attics, and floor-standing lamps all camp out under the café's arched ceilings. Montmartre is best saved for an evening visit, when locals cram in for animated conversation.

Řetězová 7, • Staré Město, • 222 221 143 • Metro: Staroměstská, Můstek • Tram: 17, 18

■ SAVOY

Found in Malá Strana, the Savoy is one of the smartest cafés in Prague. Marble-topped tables, an opulent neo-Renaissance ceiling, and one room decorated solely with wine bottles all go to make a visit here one of relaxed elegance. It is packed from opening to closing time with Praguers enjoying breakfast, lunch, an afternoon coffee, or a glass of wine.

Vítězná 5, • http://cafesavoy.ambi.cz • 257 311 562 • Metro: Můstek • Tram: 22

The Grand Café Orient's restored cubist-style interior provides an elegant setting for a coffee break.

◼ LOUVRE

Still one of the best loved cafés in Prague, Nové Město's Louvre buzzes with activity from morning until night. An ornate interior with high ceilings, tall windows, and mirrors make for a somewhat regal café experience. Situated on the main route between Wenceslas Square (Václavské náměstí) and Legionnaires Bridge (Most Legií), the café occupies an upper floor and has a small outdoor area, a billiards hall, and gallery.

Národní 22 • www.cafelouvre.cz • 224 930 949 • Metro: Národní třída, Můstek

◼ SLAVIA

Opened in the late 1880s, Nové Město's Slavia today hangs onto its reputation from the 1920s, when Prague's writers and artists came here to hash over the cultural news of the day. During the communist era, the café was a favorite of playwright (and later president) Václav Havel. Though the café lacks some of its original charm, a window seat here overlooking the Vltava River provides a good spot to pass an afternoon.

Smetanovo nábřeží 2, • www.cafeslavia.cz • 224 218 493 • Metro: Národní třída, Můstek

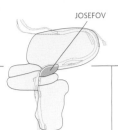

Josefov

Today, when you wander into the former Jewish quarter, you may not realize you've entered a distinct district as it's surrounded on three sides by Staré Město. Founded in the Middle Ages—and named Josefov for Habsburg emperor Josef II—the Jewish ghetto was a teeming tangle of narrow lanes, disease-ridden living quarters, synagogues, and workshops, ever subject to pogroms, until the late 19th century, when the Habsburg authorities set about tearing down much of it in order to establish broad, Parisian-style streets. Today, elegant, art nouveau apartment buildings rub shoulders with the Old Jewish Cemetery and the few remaining synagogues and halls that now form the Jewish Museum (Židovské muzeum). The district is also home to the Rudolfinum concert hall, the Museum of Decorative Arts, and the 13th-century Convent of St. Agnes, whose cloisters house a rich collection of medieval art.

◐ **The former Ceremonial Hall now diplays part of the Jewish Museum's collection.**

Josefov

One of Europe's most complete former Jewish quarters, the area has lovingly restored synagogues and stately cultural halls.

❶ Rudolfinum (see p. 76) This former Czech Parliament building is now home to the Czech Philharmonic. Take in its neoclassical fin-de-siècle grandeur and enjoy an art show in the gallery. Cross Křižovnická.

❷ Museum of Decorative Arts (see pp. 76–77) Showcasing the best of Bohemian design and craft, the museum displays include glass, jewelry, clocks, and textiles. Walk south on Křižovnická and turn left onto Široká.

❹ Ceremonial Hall (see p. 79) This pseudo-Romanesque hall has Renaissance-style interior decorations. Once you've looked around its displays on traditional burial customs, enter the building to your right.

❺ Klausen Synagogue (see p. 80) The spare, whitewashed arches within this temple frame a series of exhibits on Jewish family life and customs. Walk east on Červená.

JOSEFOV

Vltava

CÉCHŮV MOST
DVOŘÁKOVO NÁBŘEŽÍ
DUŠNÍ
17. LISTOPADU
PAŘÍŽSKÁ

Museum of Decorative Arts
(Uměleckoprůmyslové muzeum)

Ceremonial Hall
(Obřadní síň)

Old-New Synagogue
(Staronová synagoga)

Rudolfinum ❶ ❷ ❹ ❻

OLD JEWISH CEMETERY
(STARÝ ŽIDOVSKÝ HŘBITOV)

Pinkas Synagogue & Old Jewish Cemetery
(Pinkasova synagoga & Starý židovský hřbitov)

Klausen Synagogue
(Klausová synagoga) ❸

Jewish Town H
(Židovs radnice) ❼

NÁMĚSTÍ JANA PALACHA

KŘIŽOVNICKÁ

Staroměstská

Maisel Synagogue
(Maiselova synagoga) ❽

KAPROVA

❸ Pinkas Synagogue & Old Jewish Cemetery (see pp. 77–79) Study the Pinkas Synagogue's memorial to Holocaust victims from Bohemia and Moravia. Then take a walk around the adjacent cemetery filled with gravestones from the 15th to 18th centuries. Exit onto Červená and turn left.

JOSEFOV   DISTANCE: 2 MILES (3.2 KM)
TIME: APPROX. 6 HOURS   METRO START: STAROMĚSTSKÁ

JOSEFOV

⑩ Convent of St. Agnes (see pp. 84–85) This former convent hosts the National Gallery's collection of medieval art.

0 — 200 meters
0 — 200 yards

NA FRANTIŠKU

ŠTEFÁNIKŮV MOST

Convent of St. Agnes
(Klášter sv. Anežky České) ⑩

RÁSNOVKA

REVOLUČNÍ

HASTALSKÁ

VĚZEŇSKÁ

⑨
Spanish Synagogue
(Španělská synagoga)

DLOUHÁ

KOZÍ

DUŠNÍ

⑨ Spanish Synagogue (see pp. 82–83) Enjoy a spectacular interior in this dashing, Moorish-style temple. Walk to the end of Vězeňská and turn left onto Kozí.

⑦ Jewish Town Hall (see p. 81) Solve the puzzle of the backward-running clock on this sturdy rococo building next to the Old-New Synagogue. Walk south on Maiselova.

⑥ Old-New Synagogue (see pp. 80–81) Soak up the atmosphere in the district's oldest intact Gothic structure, dating from 1270. Cross the road.

⑧ Maisel Synagogue (see p. 82) Look around examples of Jewish art and history in this opulent hall. Then walk back up Maiselova and turn right onto Široká. Continue on Vězeňská.

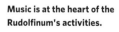

JOSEFOV

Rudolfinum

1 The civic pride that went into this grandiose 19th-century cultural center is evident in the walnut paneling, crystal windows, and glowing glass lamps that decorate the interior. From 1919, the building served as the young Czechoslovakia's legislative heart until the Nazis closed the parliament in 1938. The newly added bronze statue of Antonín Dvořák standing in front signals the Rudolfinum's current role as Prague's leading concert hall. Enter the building up the sweeping front steps to find the concert hall, which holds concerts on some mornings as well as evenings. This warm-colored, balconied space faces a stage dominated by glorious organ pipes. The seats on either side of the organ are the cheapest and allow you to gaze directly down on the orchestra—if you're not too shy to be almost sharing the stage with the musicians. Enter the building from the riverside entrance and pass through the soaring atrium to reach the Rudolfinum **Art Gallery.** This series of narrow, parquet-floored halls on two floors hosts temporary exhibitions of international art, from Chinese meta-political paintings to Persian eroticism. Don't miss the Old-Europe-style café at the east end of the atrium, set off by dignified darkwood pillars.

Music is at the heart of the Rudolfinum's activities.

Alšovo nábřeží 12, Prague 1 • www.ceskafilharmonie.cz • 227 059 205 • Gallery: $, closed Mon. • Metro: Staroměstská • Tram: 17, 18

Museum of Decorative Arts

2 Founded in 1885 in part to celebrate the wonders of the Industrial Age, the Museum of Decorative Arts (Uměleckoprůmyslové muzeum) is a treasure-house of handcrafted work. Spanning the Middle Ages through to the 20th century, the exhibits include Bohemian crystal, porcelain, clocks and watches, textiles, fashion, furnishings, photography, and graphic art, although only a small proportion of the museum's vast collection is on display at any one time.

The three levels of wonders begin with the staircase topped by sculpted arches, which rises above an art bar café and a gift shop. Upstairs, in corridors lit by floor-to-ceiling arched windows and dotted with the odd art nouveau stained-glass window, the permanent collection is organized by materials. The Story of Fiber features rich, courtly textiles and 1920s' fashion, while Print & Image shows the outstanding Czech tradition of photography and graphic art. In the Time Machines room to the left of the stairs as you come up, look for the Popper desk clock, an 18th-century Viennnese marble-and-mahogany piece.

17. listopadu 2, Prague 1 • www.upm.cz • 251 093 111 • $ • Closed Mon. • Metro: Staroměstská • Tram: 17, 18

One of several stained-glass windows in the **Museum of Decorative Arts**

Pinkas Synagogue & Old Jewish Cemetery

③ A visit to the Jewish Museum (Židovské muzeum; see sidebar p. 79), which is spread over six sites in Josefov, usually begins at the Pinkas Synagogue (Pinkasova synagoga), whose Renaissance-style interior houses the **Holocaust Memorial** commemorating the Jews from all over Bohemia and Moravia who perished. In all, around 78,000

The names of Czech victims of the Holocaust are handwritten on the walls of the Pinkas Synagogue.

names—organized by community and in families from the oldest member to the youngest—cover the interior walls. Upstairs, the exhibition **Children's Drawings from Terezín 1942–1944** shows drawings and paintings by some of the 10,000 or more children interned at the Terezín concentration camp near Prague. Many were moved on to Auschwitz and most never returned.

Squeezed between the Pinkas and Klausen Synagogues lies the **Old Jewish Cemetery** (Starý židovský hřbitov). Within its high walls, built to keep out onlookers, nearly 12,000 densely packed gravestones fairly topple over each other amid a scattering of spindly trees. Each tombstone is decorated with a carved symbolic figure representing the family interred, the carved Hebrew characters fading with time as moss grows across their granite surfaces. Look for the lion marking the gravestone of Rabbi Loew (see sidebar p. 80) next to the path on the cemetery's west side. Burials took place here from the early 15th century until 1787, when the city authorities allowed the Jewish community to acquire additional burial sites in the city. By then, so many people had been laid to rest in the cemetery that they were layered 12 deep.

Široká 3, Prague 1 • www.jewishmuseum.cz • 222 749 211 • Closed Sat. and Jewish holidays • Metro: Staroměstská • Tram: 17, 18

Ceremonial Hall

4 Within this curvaceous yet forbiddingly fortress-like building, constructed in 1911–1912 and formerly known as the Ceremonial Hall (Obřadní síň) of the Prague Burial Society, or Chevra kadisha (founded in 1564), you can find part of the Jewish Museum's permanent exhibition on Jewish customs and traditions. Appropriately, the rituals associated with treating illness and dealing with death are the focus here, with displays on burial and cleansing rituals, alms cups, together with items—from ballot boxes to dignified oil paintings of its elite members—that show off the former status of the once-important Burial Society.

The hall itself is richly ornamented with mosaic patterned floors, coffee-colored walls decorated with stenciled tracery, and leaded-glass windows that bathe the rooms in a permanently diffused and melancholy light. In all, the interior conveys some sense of the splendor that went hand-in-hand with the poverty and overcrowding of the ghetto before it was leveled to make way for Josefov's Paris-style boulevards.

U starého hřbitova 3a, Prague 1 • www.jewishmuseum.cz • 222 317 191 • Closed Sat. and Jewish holidays • Metro: Staroměstská • Tram: 17, 18

Klausen Synagogue

5 Another survivor of the ghetto clearance, the late 17th-century Klausen Synagogue (Klausová synagoga) still stands proud as the temple that held the honor of largest synagogue in the community. These days its baroque nave, surrounded by double-arched glass windows and delicately detailed, floral-patterned vaulting, hosts another part of the Jewish Museum's exhibition on customs and traditions, this time focusing on religious practices, everyday life, and the customs surrounding birth, circumcision, bar mitzvahs, weddings, and divorce. The paintings depicting deathbed duties and grave rituals of the Prague Burial Society bring a touch of somberness to the elegant interior.

IN THE **KNOW**

Rabbi Loew—or to give him his full name, Judah Loew ben Bezalel—was born around 1520. A scholar and philosopher, he was chief rabbi of Prague and officiated at the Old-New Synagogue. In the 19th century, he became the subject of the legend of the Golem, a folklore figure made from clay. The story went that he had made and animated a Golem to protect the ghetto from attack.

U starého hřbitova 3a, Prague 1 • www.jewishmuseum.cz • 221 711 511 • Closed Sat. and Jewish holidays • Metro: Staroměstská • Tram: 17, 18

Old-New Synagogue

6 Although not part of the Jewish Museum, this historic treasure is the most remarkable religious site in the district and one of Bohemian architecture's great surviving gems. Originally known as the New Synagogue, it became the Old-New Synagogue (Staronová synagoga) when another synagogue was built nearby. It is probably the only building in Prague that has been in continuous use since the 13th century, and today is one of just three synagogues in the city that still hold religious services. Hunkered down on a corner opposite the upscale Pařížská shopping boulevard, this spare, Gothic synagogue with its signature stepped brick gables is still at the heart of Jewish worship in Prague. Within, its riches are even more apparent, although understated: After passing under carved grape clusters and vine-leaf motifs above the entrance portal, you enter a moody double-nave sanctuary lit by suspended iron candelabras and enclosed by five-ribbed vaulting overhead—a feature said to be unique to local master builders. Medieval furnishings are all around, including stone pews and a late 15th-century filigreed ironwork grille surrounding the *almemar,* the central platform where the rabbi reads from the Torah scrolls during services.

Maiselova 18, Prague 1 • www.synagogue.cz • 224 800 812 • $$ • Closed Sat. and Jewish holidays • Metro: Staroměstská • Tram: 17, 18

Jewish Town Hall

7 Still actively administering the Prague Jewish community, the Jewish Town Hall (Židovská radnice) is a testament to the revival of what was once one of Bohemia's most vital ethnic populations. Unless you have town hall business, you can only view the exterior, but its features are nonetheless noteworthy. The building has stood here, on the corner of tiny Červená ulice, since 1586. The legendary mayor Mordecai Maisel, for whom the street is named, commissioned the hall, and its main curiosity is its pair of clocks. The conventional clockface on the tower shows standard time; the lower clockface, with Hebrew characters, embedded in the swooping pantiles of the roof runs backward. The seemingly contradictory motion of the lower clock makes sense when you remember that Hebrew characters, which double as letters and numbers, are read from right to left, explaining the clock's counterclockwise motion.

Maiselova 18, Prague 1 • Metro: Staroměstská • Tram: 17, 18

One of the Jewish Town Hall's clocks has Hebrew characters.

JOSEFOV

GOOD **EATS**

■ DINITZ

Prague's leading kosher restaurant appeals to all faiths with excellent variations on hummus, Middle Eastern salads, tender Brazilian steak, house specials, and Sabbath meals cooked to perfection.
Bílkova 12, 222 244 000, $$$

■ KOLONIAL

This cozy café with its unusual bicycling theme is a local favorite offering great breakfast options from 8 a.m. weekdays—its strudel is a must. It serves Mediterranean cuisine until midnight.
Široká 6, 224 818 322, $$–$$$

■ V KOLKOVNĚ

Duck, pork, sauerkraut, and dumplings alongside pleasantly bitter Pilsner Urquell beer are on offer in this buzzingly retro pub restaurant. V Kolkovně 8, 224 819 701, $$$

Maisel Synagogue

8 In some ways the grandest of the six surviving synagogues in Josefov, the Maisel Synagogue (Maiselova synagoga), with its whitewashed, twin-portal courtyard and elaborate rose window facing the street, hosts the Jewish Museum's most complete exhibition. Here you can find out about the history of Jewish settlements in Bohemia and Moravia from the 10th century to their emancipation under Habsburg emperor Joseph II in the 18th century. Medieval Hebrew manuscripts, sacred ceremonial objects, silver cups, coins, and other items convey some of the richness and diversity that once marked these communities. Oddly squeezed in between two apartment blocks, the building's pseudo-Gothic appearance dates from a major makeover during the ghetto clearance. The only surviving traces of the original Renaissance layout is the central hall's tripartite ground plan and the women's gallery on the upper floor.

Maiselova 18, Prague 1 • www.jewishmuseum.cz • Closed Sat. and Jewish holidays • Metro: Staroměstská • Tram: 17, 18

Spanish Synagogue

9 Fabulously designed in the Moorish style that was popular in the late 19th century, the Spanish Synagogue (Španělská synagoga) owes its look more to fashion than to any Sephardic heritage. Yet, with its elegant yellow-and-white exterior, keyhole arches, green-colored domed turrets, and triangular roof gables, it would look at home in any Spanish castle city. Inside, the dizzying profusion of patterns covering meticulously restored domes and arches, the vibrant copper and turquoise color accents, and the

Gilded stuccowork and stylized geometric and floral patterns cover every inch of the Spanish Synagogue's interior.

gleaming organ pipes provide a lush architectural experience. The upper galleries house displays on the history of the Jews from emancipation in the 18th century to the Holocaust. The synagogue is the place to catch great early-evening concerts of traditional Jewish music *(www.pragueticket office.com)*. At the back of the synagogue, the **Robert Guttmann Gallery** *(U staré školy 3, www.jewish museum.cz, $)* shows well-curated Jewish art from around the world.

U staré školy 1, Prague 1 • www.jewishmuseum.cz • 222 749 211 • Closed Sat. and Jewish holidays • Metro: Staroměstská • Tram: 17, 18

Convent of St. Agnes

10 See pp. 84–85.

U Milosrdných 17, Prague 1 • www.ngprague.cz • 224 810 628 • $ • Closed Mon. • Metro: Staroměstská • Tram: 17, 18

Convent of St. Agnes

Austere, unadorned buildings combine with richly textured artwork to make this National Gallery site a double treasure.

The convent's permanent collection of medieval art includes several large altarpieces.

Founded in 1231 by Agnes, sister of King Wenceslas I, the Convent of St. Agnes (Klášter sv. Anežky České) houses the National Gallery's extensive collection of medieval art of Bohemia and central Europe. Alongside a spindly, stone-walled church and other former convent buildings, a series of halls present mainly Czech art from the 14th to early 16th centuries, including statues, panel paintings, and altarpieces. Much of the work is by unknown artists; they are referred to by the name of the town where they worked.

■ BOHEMIAN GOTHIC

The first set of rooms, up a set of worn sandstone stairs, house a moodily lit collection of altarpieces, carved Madonnas, and statues of saints—many pockmarked by the attentions of hungry woodworms—that reflect the animated, Gothic painting style of the Reims School in France or the realism of sculptor and architect Peter Parler. Mid-14th-century gems include the Italian-influenced **Madonna of Vyšehrad** and the haunting panel painting of the **Ascension of Christ** from the Vyšší Brod Altarpiece. The later, chilling, red-drenched **Resurrection** from the Master of Třeboň Altarpiece (1380) shows the influence of International Gothic.

■ MASTER THEODORIC

A mysterious figure in the Bohemian Gothic art world, Theodoric was a favorite painter of the 14th-century emperor Charles IV. He created nearly 130 portraits for the emperor's summer palace in Karlštejn, just south of Prague. Six of the protraits are now on display here and show the stylistic features—neckless, claw-handed figures with

IN **THE KNOW**

Many visitors head straight for the art treasures, taking little notice of the spare, echoing former convent to the right of the main entrance. Before you immerse yourself in the richness of the sacred art, it's worth wandering the double-nave **Church of St. Francis** with its 120-foot-high (37 m) gables, the ambulatory, the refectory, and the brick-vaulted chamber where Agnes lived.

soft but courageous expressions—as if listening to angels whispering in their ears—that characterize his work and distinguish these portraits from others produced in Europe at the time.

■ GRAND TRIPTYCHS

The final exhibition space provides up-close looks at multipanel altarpieces that most congregations never got near. With dire warnings of demons on one side, crowds rising from the dead in the center panel, and hosts of surreal angels on the right, these works form a set of object lessons meant to terrify and instil wonder into the earthy peasants of Bohemia. None does this better than the epic **Holy Trinity** by the Master of Litoměřice.

JOSEFOV

U Milosrdných 17, Prague 1 • www.ngprague.cz • 224 810 628 • $ • Closed Mon. • Metro: Staroměstská • Tram: 17, 18

Jewish Heritage

Some historical accounts date the arrival of Jewish settlers in the lands that later became Bohemia to before A.D. 33, well before the arrival of the Slavs from Asia in the 8th century. In the 12th century, Prague's Jews founded a Jewish town in Staré Město and the community grew into one of the largest in Europe. Until the Holocaust, it formed a pillar of Czechoslovakian society.

A bronze statue of Jewish writer Franz Kafka, who was born and lived in Prague, outside the Spanish Synagogue. Opposite: The Old Jewish Cemetery

Oppression and Emancipation

Following Emperor Joseph II's emancipation of the Jewish community in 1781, the former ghetto was named Josefov in his honor. In earlier times, the teeming population had been confined to this one area of narrow streets and tightly packed houses. In the late 16th and early 17th centuries, the situation changed a little when Emperor Rudolf II employed Mayor Mordecai Maisel, leader and benefactor of the Jewish community at that time, as his banker and included leading Jewish scholars among his retainers.

By the start of the ghetto clearance in 1893, many Jewish families had moved out. The community saved the cemetery, synagogues, and other buildings that make up the Jewish Museum (see sidebar p. 79) and some of their most valuable contents.

Twentieth-century Holocaust

Following the German annexation of Czechoslovakia in 1938, the Nazis introduced anti-Semitic legislation. In September 1941, Reinhard Heydrich, a key architect of the Final Solution,

JOSEFOV

became governor of Bohemia and Moravia, and deportations began to the concentration camp at Terezín (formerly Theresienstadt), 35 miles (56 km) north of Prague. Around 45,500 Jews from Prague were deported, and are among those commemorated at the Pinkas Synagogue (Pinkasova synagoga; see pp. 77–78).

Modern Revival

In 1994, the Jewish Museum was returned to the Jewish community. Only the Old-New Synagogue (Staronová synagoga; see pp. 80–81) has revived worship services in Josefov, although the Spanish Synagogue (Španělská synagoga; see pp. 82–83) holds Sabbath eve meetings. The Jewish Community of Prague (*www.kehilaprague.cz*) supports Holocaust survivors and fights for the return of vast property stolen during World War II.

SYNAGOGUE TERMS

Almemar: The raised platform at the center of the synagogue where the rabbi reads from the Torah.

Aron ha-kodesh: The ark, usually concealed behind decorative curtains at the front of the temple.

Chumash: The method of binding together the five books of the Torah used for weekly readings.

Mehitzah: The screen that divides off the women's area in Orthodox synagogues that have no separate gallery.

Yad: The silver pointer in the shape of a hand with extended index finger for reading from the Torah.

JOSEFOV

Neighborhood Shopping

Since the early 20th century, when Praguers adopted modernist styles, bold art movements, and haute couture from Paris, the city has been a haven for seekers of exceptional style. Savvy shoppers search out fashion, glass, porcelain, garnets, jewelry, and all-around excellence in craftsmanship.

■ PRAGUE STYLE

The few blocks east from Josefov's Pařížská street and south from Široká have become the city's mecca for haute couture. Since the 1990s, Czech designers have opened a half dozen intimate boutiques that would hold their own against anything in London or New York. **Tatiana** (*Dušní 1, Prague 1, www.tatiana.cz, 224 813 723, closed Sun.*), featuring designs by Tat' íana Kovaříková, who has exhibited in the Museum of Decorative Arts, boasts sleek women's wear made from top-quality fabrics doted on by Czech celebs and politicos.

Nearby **Boheme** (*Dušní 8, Prague 1, www.boheme.cz, 224 813 840, closed Sun.*) offers chic monochrome ensembles and separates, while **Studio Hana Havelkova** (*Dušní 10, Prague 1, www.havelkova.com, 222 326 754*) claims influences from cubism, functionalism, constructivism, and the Bauhaus. **Navarila** (*Elišky Krásnohorské 4, Prague 1, www.navarila.cz, 271 742 091*), meanwhile, addresses a younger clientele with retro 1970s'-style knits employing a provocative color palette.

Gents need not feel left out when boulevarding in Prague, thanks to the fine-felt traditional haberdashery work of **Tonak** tucked into a corner of the Koruna Palace arcade in Nové Město (*Wenceslas Square 1, Prague 1, www.tonak.cz, 420 224 218 506*).

■ CRYSTAL CLEAR

Longtime Prague resident, expat-American Karen Feldman, wanted to combine the best of traditional Czech glass craft with designs that appeal to stylistas—thus, her design shop **Artěl** (*Celetná 29, Prague 1, www.artelglass.com, 224 815 085*) in Staré Město. The pieces she sells reconceive mouth-blown fine crystal by combining it with

Artěl sells a mix of innovative glassware, antiques, and quirky accessories and household items.

etching and cutting patterns that are fresh, yet classic, thanks to the work of a new generation of Czech artists. But have no fear, the 19th-century Bohemian standard-bearer **Moser** (*Na Příkopě 12, Prague 1, www.moser-glass.com, 221 890 891*), on the border of Staré Město and Nové Město, is still alive and well, selling fine crystal the like of which you can find in palaces all over Europe.

■ JEWEL IN THE CROWN

Czech master traditions in gem-cutting and jewelry-making date back to the Middle Ages, but the latest wave of designers are just as engaged in creating unique adornments. In a new generation of shops, like Staré Město's **PARAZIT** (*Karlova 25, Prague 1, www.parazit.cz, 731 171 517, closed Sun.*), which serve as designer collectives, you can find treasures such as the whimsical deer-themed creations of Jelení.

Classic Czech garnets were essential wear for centuries of Bohemian kings and queens. Today, the semi-precious stones are visible everywhere in Prague shops. The small red gems are usually worked into silver or gold settings that form geometric or floral shapes or the occasional enchanted forest animal. The grandaddy of them all, the formerly state-run **Granát Turnov** (*Dlouhá 28, Prague 1, www.granat.eu, 222 315 612*), has an official outlet in Staré Město, though there's not much price or quality difference in the stones. Antique settings, such as you might find at Josefov's **Art Deco** (*Kozí 9, Prague 1, www.artdecoprague.com, 224 815 848*), are among the most appealing and interesting.

■ MUSEUM QUALITY FOR THE HOME
The **Hard de Core Gallery** (*Senovážné nám. 10, Prague 1, www.harddecore.cz, 775 417 230, closed Sun.*) in an easily overlooked shopping passage in Staré Město is worth seeking out. Its remarkable array of fresh creations by up-and-coming designers include František Vízner's modernist wine glasses, Petr Bakos' cool, dart-shaped lampshades, and angular porcelain sweet boats by Alžběta Zimmerová.

Cubism, a Czech obsession, does not just take the form of architecture. It can transform something as quotidian as a teapot into a fantastic work of art. Head to Staré Město's **Kubista** on the ground floor of the House of the Black Madonna (see p. 60), where cubist-style, Prague-only items made of metal,

paper, fabric, ceramics, and glass and furnishings—including reproductions of pieces from the 1920s and 1930s—may force you to push your carry-on luggage to the limit.

Czech Porcelain (Český porcelán; *Perlová 1, Prague 1, www.ceskyporcelan .cz, 224 210 995, closed Sun.*) in Staré Město is best known for its traditional Bohemian, rococo-style, Blue Onion porcelain produced at its factory in Dubí, northwest Bohemia. The shop sells a large range of products, from ceramic house numbers, mugs, and plant pots to full dinner services in Blue Onion and several other patterns.

■ CRAFTS ON A STRING
Puppetry is a Czech tradition dating back to the baroque era, when marionette theaters were all the rage and master craftsmen created versatile and maneuverable figures that seemed to take on lives of their own. The open markets of Havelská are filled with puppets, but most are factory made and not built to last. Thus, the artists who founded **Truhlář Marionettes** (Marionety Truhlář; *U Lužického semináře 5., Prague 1, www.marionety .com*) set themselves apart with lovingly handcrafted puppets in whimsical forms that could only have come from this group of artist-carpenters.

Truhlář's traditional hand-carved wooden puppets come in a range of sizes.

Truhlář's quaint rustic workshop, which sits just downstream of the Charles Bridge in Malá Strana, is easy to spot. Nowhere else will you see windows filled with witches, wizards, gnomes, and dragons that look anything like this. Better still, Saturday courses under the guidance of Pavel Truhlář provide the opportunity to try creating your own puppet.

■ TRADITIONAL PRODUCTS
Handmade toys, kitchenware, ceramics, and household objects that might have come from a timeless Czech village fill the shelves and aisles of

Manufaktura (*Mostecká 17, Prague 1, www.manufaktura.cz, 230 234 376*). This chain of shops includes branches in Malá Strana and Staré Město—there's even one at the airport lest you forget to buy that special gift until the last moment. Favorites are invariably the stuffed Krtek dolls, the personification of the classic cartoon mole of children's fairy tales. They were the creation of Zdeněk Miler, who entertained generations with the curious creature's adventures. Soaps scented with local herbs, lotions, candles, and eco-friendly cosmetics are almost as popular.

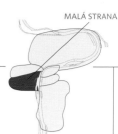

Malá Strana

Stretching along the left bank of the Vltava River from Prague Castle to the base of Petřín Hill, Malá Strana (Lesser or Little Quarter) is a slower-paced, more idyllic counterpart to Staré Město. A settlement sprung up here, below the castle, in the 13th century, but fire destroyed much of it in 1541, making way for a wave of baroque makeovers unmatched in Europe for technical flourishes and variety. Narrow streets with colorful, highly decorative facades lead to aristocratic palaces and the finest baroque church in the city. But for all its stateliness, this small quarter is filled with anachronisms. A mirror maze created in 1891 greets riders of the Petřín Hill funicular railway, as does the pre-World War II Štefánik Observatory. And some very 20th-century graffiti adorns part of a well-preserved 18th-century square that was chosen by native son Milos Forman as a setting for his film *Amadeus* in 1984.

◀ **The two-story Philosophical Hall, part of the Strahov Monastery's library**

Malá Strana

This district of palaces, gardens, pubs, coffeeshops, workshops, and miles of cobblestone lanes was where the real Bohemians lived.

1 Malá Strana Bridge Tower (see p. 96) Dating from 1464, the Gothic tower on the Charles Bridge's Malá Strana side provides a ceremonious arrival for left-bank walkers. Turn right just past the tower.

2 U Lužického Semináře (see pp. 96–97) Stroll through time in this medieval warren of smithies, stables, and boat ramps. Turn left onto Letenská and look for a doorway in the wall on the right.

3 Wallenstein Palace (see p. 97) Enjoy Habsburg General Albrecht von Wallenstein's baroque gardens, complete with fashionable faux grotto. Leave via Wallenstein Square (Valdštejnský náměstí) to reach Nerudova.

10 Strahov Monastery (see pp. 104–107) Tour the monastery and its two ornately baroque libraries, and enjoy a spectacular view of the city.

9 Petřín Hill (see p. 103) One of the city's few perfect destinations for kids (and kissers), this hill has a mirror maze, an observatory, and a mini Eiffel Tower. Follow the path northwest toward Strahov and go to the main entrance at the western end of the monastery.

ÚVOZ

DLABAČOV

Strahov Monastery (Strahovský klášter)

10

STRAHOVSKÁ ZAHRADA

SCHÖNBORNSKÁ ZAHRADA

LOBKOVICKÁ ZAHRADA

MALÁ STRANA

Hladová zeď'

Petřín Hill (Petřín)

9

Petřín Tower (Petřínská rozhledna)

PETŘÍNSKÉ SADY

0 — 400 meters
0 — 400 yards

MALÁ STRANA   DISTANCE: 2 MILES (3.2 KM)
TIME: APPROX. 6 HOURS   METRO START: STAROMĚSTSKÁ

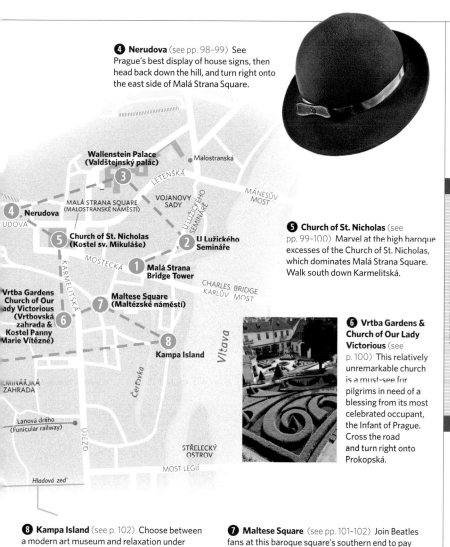

4 **Nerudova** (see pp. 98–99) See Prague's best display of house signs, then head back down the hill, and turn right onto the east side of Malá Strana Square.

Wallenstein Palace
(Valdštejnský palác)

Malostranská

3

LETENSKÁ

MÁNESŮV MOST

MALÁ STRANA SQUARE
(MALOSTRANSKÉ NÁMĚSTÍ)

VOJANOVY SADY

U LUŽICKÉHO SEMINÁŘE

4 Nerudova

UDOVA

5 **Church of St. Nicholas**
(Kostel sv. Mikuláše)

2 **U Lužického**
Semináře

MOSTECKÁ

1 **Malá Strana**
Bridge Tower

CHARLES BRIDGE
KARLŮV MOST

KARMELITSKÁ

Vrtba Gardens &
Church of Our
Lady Victorious
(Vrtbovská
zahrada &
Kostel Panny
Marie Vítězné)

6

7 **Maltese Square**
(Maltézské náměstí)

Vltava

8 **Kampa Island**

Čertovka

EMINÁŘSKÁ
ZAHRADA

Lanová dráha
(Funicular railway)

ÚJEZD

STŘELECKÝ
OSTROV

MOST LEGIÍ

Hladová zeď'

5 **Church of St. Nicholas** (see pp. 99–100) Marvel at the high baroque excesses of the Church of St. Nicholas, which dominates Malá Strana Square. Walk south down Karmelitská.

6 **Vrtba Gardens & Church of Our Lady Victorious** (see p. 100) This relatively unremarkable church is a must-see for pilgrims in need of a blessing from its most celebrated occupant, the Infant of Prague. Cross the road and turn right onto Prokopská.

8 **Kampa Island** (see p. 102) Choose between a modern art museum and relaxation under the trees on this grassy spit of land by the river. Return to Karmelitská and take the funicular up Petřín Hill.

7 **Maltese Square** (see pp. 101–102) Join Beatles fans at this baroque square's southern end to pay tribute to an act of pre-1989 dissidence—the spray-painting of John Lennon's image on a church wall. Stroll into the park.

Malá Strana Bridge Tower

1 A wedge-shaped mansard tower with four pinnacles rises above this stout structure on the Malá Strana end of the Charles Bridge (see pp. 54–55). Delicate tracery adorns the tower, whose walls are made of brick and stone. The Malá Strana tower was originally Romanesque in style, but in 1464, inspired by Peter Parler's Staré Město Bridge Tower, Bohemian king George of Poděbrady had the Gothic form visible today layered onto the original building—a common practice among thrifty Czechs. A **museum** in the Malá Strana tower houses an exhibition on the role of the Charles Bridge in Prague's history. The **viewing platform** at the top of the tower provides excellent views of the city.

Mostecká, Prague 1 • www.muzeumprahy.cz
• 221 714 575 • $ • Metro: Malostranská
• Tram: 20, 22

A stone gateway links the Malá Strana bridge tower on the right to the older Judita bridge tower.

U Lužického Semináře

2 This assemblage of baroque town houses, galleries, pubs, riverside eateries, and shops form a quiet gem of a square. Only a dozen buildings surround the little triangle of grass, but they include **Shakespeare & Sons,** a secondhand bookshop beloved by expats. It sells English-language translations of Czech classics. You can also visit centuries-old watering holes, a small walled garden—**Vojan Park** (Vojanovy sady)—with peacocks and palatial fountain, and calming riverside restaurants. The smartest of these eateries, Hergetova Cihelna, shares a building with the **Kafka Museum** (*Cihelná 2b, www.kafkamuzeum.cz, 296 826 103, $$*) dedicated to Prague's most celebrated writer, Franz Kafka (see sidebar right). His journals and correspondence together with little-known photographs fill the museum's dimly lit halls.

U Lužického semináře, Prague I • Metro: Malostranská • Tram: 20, 22

Wallenstein Palace

3 Go through the door in the high, blank wall on Letenská to find the gardens of the Wallenstein Palace (Valdštejnský palác), the former residence of Albrecht von Wallenstein. In the 17th century, Wallenstein led the Catholic armies of the Counter-Reformation on behalf of Habsburg Emperor Ferdinand II in putting down a force of Bohemian Protestants. The palace was his reward, along with the magnificent garden. At the eastern end of the garden, the windows of the former riding school, now converted into the **Wallenstein Gallery** (*www.ngprague.cz, $, closed Mon.*), overlook an ornamental duck pond. The gallery puts on large-scale temporary shows celebrating Central European history. To the west, bronze statues line formal pathways leading to a colonnaded garden pavilion. Beyond that is the palace, which now houses the Senate of the Czech Republic, whose reception rooms are open to the public on weekends. The two-story **Main Hall** is decorated with exquisite stuccowork and frescoes in the early baroque style. The open stage at the garden's south end hosts free summer concerts.

Valdštejnské náměstí 4, Prague 1 • 257 075 707 • Garden closed Nov.–Mar.; Senate closed Mon.–Fri. • Metro: Malostranská • Tram: 18, 20, 22

MALÁ STRANA

The sign of the House at the Golden Cup (No. 16) on Nerudova

MALÁ STRANA

Nerudova

4 Lined with elaborate high-baroque facades, this steep street—which was once embedded with wooden beams to keep beasts of burden from losing their footing—offers a rich glimpse of Prague life under Habsburg rule. The buildings, many of which are now apartment blocks, hotels, and embassies, demonstrate the rewards given by grateful emperors to royal retainers, who adorned their dwellings with statues and carvings. The exterior of the **Morzin Palace** (Morzinský palác; *No. 5),* former redoubt of Count Václav of Morzin and now the Romanian Embassy, fairly groans under the weight of sculptures by Bohemian artist Ferdinand Maximilian Brokoff, who also spruced up the Charles Bridge with statues of saints.

Another feature of Nerudova is the abundance of painted house signs—it has more than any other street in Prague. The tradition of identifying buildings using painted signs began in medieval times and continued until 1770, when the Habsburgs introduced a numbering system. Mythic figures, animals, everyday objects such as keys and cups, all appear carved or painted on building facades. Several buildings, such as **At the Red Lion**

The sign for No. 43 Nerudova, At the Green Lobster

(U Červeného lva; *No. 41*), are inns. **At the Two Suns** (U Dvou sluncü; *No. 47*), home of the 19th-century poet Jan Neruda from 1845 to 1857, now has a restaurant on the first floor where former president Václav Havel took foreign heads of state to sample Czech beer.

Nerudova, Prague 1 • Metro: Malostranská • Tram: 20, 22

Church of St. Nicholas

5 As you approach the doors to the 18th-century Church of St. Nicholas (Kostel sv. Mikuláše) on Malá Strana Square (Malostranské náměstí), notice the nearby plague column—a thank-you tribute from survivors of the pandemic of 1713–1714.

Inside the church, a complex arrangement of columns, statues, arches, filigree, frescoes, and domes challenges your visual sense. Heavily gilded details lead the eye ever upward. The nave's ceiling fresco showing St. Nick overcoming a demon competes for attention with 4,000 state-of-the-art organ pipes, some of them 20 feet (6 m) in height, and the elaborate 230-foot-high (70 m) main dome featuring a florid fresco—"Celebration of the Holy Trinity"—by Franz Palko. Designed by architects Christoph Dientzenhofer and his precocious son Kilian Ignatz, the church represents the crowning achievement of both high baroque

Natural light floods into the sumptuously decorated interior of the Church of St. Nicholas.

and epic religious art and attests to the Jesuit Order's money-no-object campaign to re-Catholicize the unruly Czech Protestants.

You can enjoy perfect views of the city from the top of the belfry—a spot favored by the secret police of the communist era for surveillance of subjects on the square below.

Malostranské náměstí, Prague 1 • www.stnicholas.cz • 257 534 215 • Closed Dec. 31 • Metro: Malostranská • Tram: 20, 22

GOOD **EATS**

■ CAFÉ SAVOY
On the district's southern border, this elegant eating spot attracts a loyal local crowd with its light continental cuisine, delicate cakes, and local wine list. Vítězná 5, Prague 5, 257 311 562, $

■ KAMPA PARK
This critically lauded waterfront dining room serves Czech classics—such as venison in juniper demi-glace—and inspired seafood dishes. Na Kampě 8b, Prague 1, 296 826 112, $$$

■ LUKA LU
The city's most authentic Balkan traditional dining room is an enchanting, cozy agglomeration of crazy decor, streetside picnic tables, and warm service. Újezd 33, Prague 1, 257 212 388, $$

Vrtba Gardens & Church of Our Lady Victorious

6 Take a relaxing stroll through Vrtba Gardens (Vrtbovská zahrada), a charming green space at the base of Petřín Hill, before tackling the **Church of Our Lady Victorious** (Kostel Panny Marie Vítězné). Thousands of visitors come to this pilgrimage center each year hoping that the church's Infant Jesus of Prague—known around the world as the Bambino di Praga—will answer their prayers. Displayed in a glass case on an altar on the right-hand side of the church, this small wooden statue of the infant Jesus was given to the Spanish bride of a member of the Lobkowicz family in 1556; she regifted it to the Barefoot Carmelites, the order of nuns whose church this is. The little figure has acquired a reputation for miraculous powers. Dressed in a different outfit each day, it is said to dispense blessings on faithful visitors who leave tributes.

Up the stairs to the right of the main altar you can find the Museum of the Infant Jesus of Prague with a display of some of the statue's many outfits and other religious objects.

Karmelitská 9, Prague 1 • www.pragjesu.info • 257 533 646 • Metro: Malostranská • Tram: 20, 22

MALÁ STRANA

Peace symbols, poems, and messages cover the John Lennon Wall.

Maltese Square

7 Eighteenth-century arches and colonnades, the Church of the Knights of Malta, a music school from which arias emanate, and the Japanese and Danish Embassies line this tranquil square (Maltézské náměstí). Former aristocratic residences around the square include the **Nostic Palace** (Nostický palác; *No. 471*) and the rococo **Turba Palace** (Turbovský palác; *No. 447*), both older buildings that were remodeled in the 1760s in rococo style.

The biggest attraction by far, though, is the graffiti-covered **John Lennon Wall** at the southern end. Psychedelic images spray-painted in tribute first appeared here following the assassination of Lennon in New York in 1980. The wall was repeatedly whitewashed on the orders of the communist authorities, but persistent fans managed to foil the cleanup crews every time and the graffiti always reappeared. Finally, the authorities gave in. To this day, people

Old houses line the narrow Čertovka millstream dividing Kampa from the rest of Malá Strana.

lovingly add new messages and lyrics to the layers of colors and enjoy, or take part in, a street performance or two.

Maltézské náměstí, Prague 1 • Metro: Malostranská • Tram: 20, 22

Kampa Island

8 Near the river, a series of small footbridges across the Čertovka millstream lead to what Praguers call the island of Kampa. The bridges are decorated with padlocks—tributes left by lovers. The island is actually a peninsula attached to the left bank at its south end, but idlers enjoying the grass, shady trees, kids' playground, and **Kampa Museum** (see p. 167) couldn't be less bothered about that. The museum features the excellent collection of Czech modernist art assembled by Czech expatriate dissidents Meda and Jan Mládek.

U Sovových mlýnů 2, Prague 1 • Metro: Malostranská • Tram: 20, 22

Petřín Hill

9 Once serving as the royal orchards that supplied Prague Castle with fresh cherries, this promontory rising west of Kampa offers some of the finest views of the city on the left bank. A counterweight-powered funicular—a classic feat of Czechnology—whisks visitors up the hill for the price of a standard tram ticket (alight just above the Újezd tram stop). The white-stone **Hunger Wall** (Hladová zed'), built in 1360–1362 as a public works project to feed the poor, runs uphill to the south. The hill's north side features an **Observation Tower** (Rozhledna; 257 320 112, $) modeled on the Eiffel Tower in tribute to Prague's cultural links with Paris. Kids are just as impressed by the **mirror maze** *(www.muzeum pradhy.cz, $)*. Built in 1891, it has distorting mirrors and a diorama of a battle between Prague citizens and a Swedish army on the Charles Bridge during the Thirty Years' War. The **Štefánik Observatory** (Štefánikova hvězdárna; *www .observatory.cz, 257 320 540, $*) opened in 1928. It offers stargazing programs in English that run afternoons and evenings year-round.

Karmelitská, Prague 1 • Metro: Malostranská • Tram: 20, 22

Strahov Monastery

10 See pp. 104–107.

Strahovské nádvoří 1, Prague 1 • www.strahovskyklaster.cz • 233 107 711 • Library $, closed Easter Day and Dec. 25; Picture Gallery and Museum of Miniatures $ • Metro: Malostranská • Tram: 22

Climb Petřín Hill Observation Tower's 299 steps for one of the best views of the city.

Strahov Monastery

The Premonstratensian Order founded the monastery in 1143 and gradually expanded it, bringing in thousands of rare books and paintings.

Stacks of rare books and a statue of St. John the Baptist occupy the library's Theological Hall.

A survivor of wars, antireligious emperors, and communist takeovers, the Strahov Monastery, its library, and picture collection are testaments to the staying power of monks dedicated to the preservation of knowledge, art . . . and great brewing technique. Through the narrow, ornate entrance archway, the monastery buildings surround a square that stretches east toward Petřín Hill. Begin with the library, on the west side of the square, followed by the church, then the gallery. The library and the gallery have their own ticket booths.

■ STRAHOV LIBRARY

The main gate of the monastery complex leads to its most celebrated feature. One of the world's most magnificent book collections—in terms of setting, if not size—fills twin halls holding some 130,000 volumes and 3,000 rare manuscripts, many in editions from before 1500.

Rich leather- and bark-bound tomes line the **Theological Hall,** which was completed in 1671 with Giovanni Domenico Orsi's ceiling frescoes of heavenly scenes. The **Philosophical Hall,** added a century later to hold the burgeoning stacks of publications available for public use, is watched over by Anton Maulbertsch's richly fanciful ceiling frescoes of 1794 depicting man's march toward wisdom. Tiers of carved walnut shelves support a wondrous compendium of medical, mathematical, geographical, and astronomical works. The **Cabinet of Curiosities,** housed in a corridor linking the two halls, holds supposed dragon fossils and other bits from mythical monsters.

In 1783, reforming emperor Joseph II, who disapproved of the Catholic Church's monastic orders, set about suppressing the monasteries throughout his lands. In a deft political maneuver, Strahov's monks convinced

IN **THE KNOW**

Beside the monastery's main entrance is the **Gallery Miro** (www.galeriemiro.cz, 233 354 066). Housed in the Renaissance Church of St. Roch, it holds temporary shows of modernist masters such as Miró, Picasso, and Dalí along with contemporary Czech artists.

him that theirs was an educational, not a religious, institution and the emperor decided to keep it open, the library thus saving the monastery.

■ CHURCH OF OUR LADY OF THE ASSUMPTION

Turn right on exiting the library to behold the sanctuary at the heart of the Strahov complex. The bells in the spires of this stunning baroque church

The cover of the so-called Codex Etchmiadzin, a rare medieval manuscript in the Strahov library

MALÁ STRANA

Curling marble columns, frescoes, and stuccowork adorn the interior of Our Lady of the Assumption.

still chime for Mass daily. The crown jewel of the Premonstratensian Order, the Church of Our Lady boasts an altarpiece supporting curling columns of locally quarried black marble. Its ceiling cartouches frame heavenly scenes of the Virgin's life by Jerzy Wilhelm Neunhertz. The loft on the west side boasts a resplendent organ, built in 1774 by the monk Lohel Oehlschlaegl, to which Mozart took a liking during his Prague stay in 1787.

■ STRAHOV PICTURE GALLERY

The entranceway to the east of the church leads through to the art collection. It would be hard to guess

from the sumptuous collections of pietàs, medieval panels, and Flemish masters in these palatial halls that the monastery's priceless holdings have been thoroughly raided over the centuries. And the Order has not forgotten that as recently as 1950, the communist government jailed priests, grabbed land, and seized church art to build up the collection of the National Gallery. With property returned after the Velvet Revolution, visitors can see works such as the 14th-century **Strahov Madonna** displayed in spaces that the monastery dubs the Romanesque Halls, a series of rooms that offer insights into centuries of simple living by the Premonstratensians. The austere **Winter Refectory,** where the monks ate basic meals in the incongruous company of a florid panel scene entitled "Heavenly Feast of the Just," contrasts with the vastly more ornate baroque **Summer Refectory.**

■ BREW WITH A VIEW

The **Strahov Gardens** stretching down toward the Vltava River form a rolling green bridge to the open spaces of Petřín Hill. The ambulatory, a rectangular path running amid the fruit trees, was once the place to spy monks walking endless laps in quiet contemplation. Now it's open to the public, and kids and couples with lunch baskets come here to enjoy the expansive view of Staré Město. Back beside the Strahov complex's main entrance you can find the monks' pride and joy—their special St. Norbert beer, named for the founder of the Premonstratensian Order. This fine, traditionally brewed beer is available on tap at Klášterni pivovar Strahov, at the tables closest to the Gallery Miro (see sidebar p. 105).

The monastery still makes and serves its own brand of beer.

Strahovské nádvoří 1, Prague 1 • www.strahovskyklaster.cz • 233 107 711 • Library $, closed Easter Day and Dec. 25; Picture Gallery and Museum of Miniatures $ • Tram: 22

Baroque Architecture

In the early 17th century, a theatrical style of architecture that incorporated elaborate decoration and surface detail became popular across Europe. The Catholic Church employed the new style to dramatic effect in its churches, and the continent's rulers and aristocracy soon followed suit. Nowhere was the baroque style taken up more enthusiastically than in Prague.

MALÁ STRANA

In the baroque era, signs rather than numbers identified Prague houses such as **At the Two Suns** (see pp. 98–99). Opposite: **Symmetrical decoration added in the early 18th century graces the facade of the 10th-century Basilica of St. George.**

Glory in Geometry

Malá Strana's **Church of Our Lady Victorious** (see p. 100) was the city's first sanctuary to be built (or rebuilt, as it was originally Renaissance in style). The word "elaborate" is hardly adequate to describe its signature baroque altar arches supported and illuminated by window arches and the gold-leaf-covered altarpiece brought in from Rome. Such features, along with richly faceted side chapels, show off classic elements of the baroque style: soaring ceilings, symmetrical proportions, imposing columns, florid paintings, and a remarkable sensuousness—visual effects that were calculated to captivate and overwhelm the congregation.

Repurposing the Sacred

Following the Reformation, the divisions between Catholics and Protestants threatened to disrupt the Catholic Habsburg dynasty's control of its empire. With the Habsburg's support, the Catholic Church in Bohemia reasserted control by imposing its own style of architecture on some of Prague's most venerated churches. Even the 10th-century Romanesque **Basilica of St. George** (see pp. 122–123) at Prague Castle was given a baroque makeover. The upgrade, designed by F. M. Kanka in the early 1700s, was cleverly done and featured a new facade featuring tidy geometric forms.

Hitting the Heights

With the conversion of the first few sacred buildings under their belt, the powers that be now needed to step up their game to win true glory. That called for a purpose-built showcase displaying every trick of false perspective in its extensive trompe l'oeil ceilings along with flowing action figures in marble. Two generations of architects would craft Prague's showboat of high baroque, the **Church of St. Nicholas** (see pp. 99–100) in Malá

BAROQUE
CHARACTERISTICS

Curvaceous feats Walls, altars, and flights of stairs appear to swirl around, showing off the dramatic impact of the form.

Extravagance Exaggerated emotion, sensory assaults, and simply conveyed messages glorify the Church and the monarchy.

Light and space The combination of spectacular natural illumination and multiple aisles allows for maximum impact.

Special effects Trompe l'oeil, a favored technique, gives flat surfaces the appearance of new depth and complexity.

MALÁ STRANA

Strana. Christoph Dientzenhoffer, the most masterful baroque practitioner in Central Europe, was assigned the job in 1703. His son Kilian Ignatz oversaw its completion 52 years later—the results still impress.

The Secular Bandwagon

Next, noble folk—always eager to show off their exquisite taste and wealth—jumped in. **Wallenstein Palace** (see p. 97) in Malá Strana was Prague's first secular baroque building. The new architectural rules and the desire to instill awe toward the aristocracy were embodied in the Knights Hall, Mythological and Astronomical Corridors, and the stately formal garden, which now forms the backyard of the Czech Senate.

Opulence Wars

Even the Wallenstein spread could be bested, of course, and competition to build the grandest estate was fierce. Starting in 1679, fashionable

Statues on the Troja Castle's garden staircase illustrate a fight between ancient gods and goddesses.

French architect Jean Baptiste Mathey built **Troja Castle** (*Trojský zámek; U Trojského zámku 1, Prague 7, www.ghmp.cz, 283 851 614, $, closed Dec.–Mar. and Mon.*) over a mere 12 years for Count Sternberg. Although the location was not as good as that of Wallenstein Palace, the estate was spacious and hilly enough to provide the palace with a backdrop of riverfront vineyards. The immense garden stairs set the tone, leading to paths lined with rare vases by Bombelli. Brothers Abraham and Isaac Godyn of Anvers created interior frescoes that are unmatched in epic scope— trompe l'oeil scenes depicting the Habsburg's deification cover every inch of the hall's walls and ceiling.

Mitteleuropean Mild

In the 18th century, architects and artists developed a lighter, even more elaborate form of baroque. The rococo style favored pastel colors and ornamentation based on natural forms. The **Colloredo-Mansfeld Palace** (Colloredo-Manfeldský palác; see p. 166) in Staré Město is a prime example of rococo. You enter

The 18th-century ballroom in the Colloredo-Mansfeld Palace features a fireplace topped by ornate carvings and flowing figures.

through a magnificent portal accented by the obligatory putti (cupids). The ballroom has extensive ceiling frescoes and an elaborate chandelier, and was used as a set in Forman's film *Amadeus*. The belfry tower atop Malá Strana's Church of St. Nicholas is another fine example of the late era of baroque.

Since the demise of communism in 1989, many of Prague's baroque palaces—which suffered neglect and disrepair for a long time—have been lovingly restored and pressed into service as galleries, museums, and hotels.

Riverside Prague

The Vltava River doesn't just divide the Czech capital, it defines a city that arguably looks its best when seen from the middle of one of its many spectacular bridges or on a riverboat trip. Stroll along the left bank in Malá Strana and you're swept along in the city's spirit—and its history.

■ BRIDGING THE DECADES

Prague's bridges serve as memorials to past glories. **Legionnaire's Bridge** (Most Legií), which connects Vítězná in Malá Strana and Národní on the southern edge of Staré Město, is a tribute to the Czech legions of World War I who turned against their Austrian commanders. The bridge also links to the small landmass in mid-river known as **Shooter's Island** (Střelecký ostrov). Newly spruced up, this green space provides a cool and calming respite during warm weather and hosts summer music festivals and open-air film screenings.

■ KAMPA INSPIRATION

The tiny **Church of St. John of the Laundry** (Sv. Jan na Prádle; *Říční and Všehrdova),* founded in 1235, attests to the role in Prague social life and history of the narrow Čertovka stream. The Knights of Malta dug out this diminutive waterway in the 12th century to separate Kampa from the rest of Malá Strana. The Little Devil, as Čertovka translates, powered mills. Two waterwheels remain, and one of them is attached to the district's popular art bar, **Tato Kojkej** *(Kampa Park, 257 323 102),* whose name is a form of nonsense Czech. With a bar created by Czech artist-provocateur David Černý, this watering hole doubles as a gallery space for up-and-coming Prague talents.

■ RIVERSIDE TRADITION

Farmers markets have taken Prague by storm. At the north end of Kampa, just past another of Černý's surreal creations—a group of giant cast babies next to the Kampa Museum—stalls set up on Saturdays, even in winter. Authentic, old-Bohemian *koláč* (pastries topped with fruit purée or cheese), *palačinky* (pancakes with sweet

The Grand Priory millwheel still turns in the waters of the Čertovka stream on Kampa Island.

or savory fillings), *kranjska klobása* (Slovenian-style pork sausages), and homemade jams draw the crowds. A block west, the waterwheel of the former **Grand Priory Mill** (*Hroznová 3*) is now home to a life-size statue of a water sprite—an ancient Bohemian folklore character—that artist Josef Nálepa installed in 2010 supposedly to help guard against flooding. The area was inundated in 2002, but, fittingly, in 2013 the antiflood fencing held up.

■ CASTING OFF

Perhaps the best way to experience Prague's temperamental river is by boat. Romantics can rent a rowboat by the hour from the concession on picturesque Slovanský Island (*$, closed Nov–March*), beside the National Theater in Nové Město. The less energetic can board a boat. The **Prague Steamship Company** (*Rašínovo nábřeží, www.paroplavba .cz, 224 930 017, $$*) offers relaxing catered cruises. True bohemians can drift along on the **Jazz Boat** (*Dvořákovo nábřeží 901, www .jazzboat.cz, 731 183 180, $$*), which features evening river cruises to the accompaniment of top performing talents.

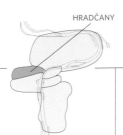

Hradčany

Overlooking the former trade route along the Vltava River, the promontory on which the compact castle district sits still dominates the Prague skyline. In the 11th century, Přemyslid rulers of Bohemia established Hradčany as their seat of power, adding churches and great vaulted halls. Czechs venerate the 14th-century Holy Roman Emperor, Charles IV, for leading Bohemia into a golden age of trade, learning, and viticulture, advances celebrated in the Story of Prague Castle exhibit. He also commissioned the Gothic gem, St. Vitus's Cathedral. In addition, the castle offers art collections, a picturesque street, and gardens.

The inclusion of Bohemia in the Habsburg empire from the 16th century onward brought fantastic wealth to Prague, funding a half dozen extravagant palaces just outside the castle gates, as well as the magnificent Loreto church and the nearby Černín Palace.

◐ Musicians entertain the crowds outside the main gates of Prague Castle.

Hradčany

Quiet backstreets vie for attention with royal palaces and ancient churches that resonate with 1,000 years of history.

① Prague Castle Picture Gallery (see p. 118)
Enter Prague Castle by the main gate. Continue into the second courtyard and turn left for the ticket office. In the gallery next door, peruse paintings by Titian, Rubens, and Tintoretto. Walk through to the third courtyard.

JELENÍ

0 — 400 meters
0 — 400 yards

HRADČANY

NOVÝ SVĚT

KEPLEROVA

Nový Svět ⑩

Prague Castle Picture Gallery
(Obrazárna Pražského hradu)

⑩ Nový Svět (see pp. 126–127)
Wander the quiet old winding lanes north of Loreto Square (Loretánské náměstí).

Hradčany Square
(Hradčanské náměstí)

Loreto Square
(Loretánské náměstí) ⑨

⑧

ÚVOZ

⑨ Loreto Square (see p. 126) Marvel at the gem-encrusted Loreto church. Walk north on Kapucínská.

⑧ Hradčany Square (see pp. 124–125) Aristocratic palaces housing some of the National Gallery's collection line this sedate square. Sample their displays, and then walk west on Loretánská.

HRADČANY   DISTANCE: 2 MILES (3.2 KM)
TIME: APPROX. 7 HOURS   METRO START: MALOSTRANSKÁ

HRADČANY

❷ Old Royal Palace (see pp. 118–119) Tour the 16th-century Vladislav Hall and other historic palace chambers. Enter the neighboring building.

❸ Story of Prague Castle (see p. 120) Find out about the castle's history, including the site's former role as a pagan burial ground and the development of the castle's fortifications. Cross the courtyard to the cathedral.

❹ St. Vitus's Cathedral (see pp. 120–122) This 1,000-year-old Gothic wonder dominating Prague's skyline is Bohemia's religious and historic heart. Walk to the far (eastern) end of the third courtyard.

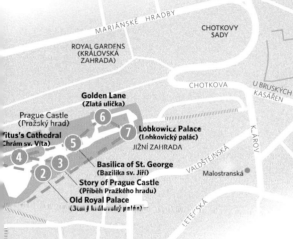

MARIÁNSKÉ HRADBY

CHOTKOVY SADY

ROYAL GARDENS (KRÁLOVSKÁ ZAHRADA)

CHOTKOVA

U BRUSKÝCH KASÁREN

Golden Lane (Zlatá ulička)

Prague Castle (Pražský hrad)

❻

Lobkowicz Palace (Lobkovický palác)

JIŽNÍ ZAHRADA

❼

K ...ROV

'itus's Cathedral hrám sv. Víta)

❺

VALDŠTEJNSKÁ

Basilica of St. George (Bazilika sv. Jiří)

Malostranská

❹ ❸

❷

Story of Prague Castle (Příběh Pražského hradu)

Old Royal Palace (Starý královský palác)

LETE... SKÁ

❼ Lobkowicz Palace (see pp. 128–129) Take in the Lobkowicz family's varied collections of art, porcelain, and historic musical scores. Leave the castle by the main gate.

❻ Golden Lane (see pp. 123–124) Breathe in the sense of former lives lived within the castle's shadow in this narrow street of cottages where re-created interiors alternate with gift shops. Return to Jiřská and turn left.

❺ Basilica of St. George (see pp. 122–123) Dating from 920, this humble Romanesque chapel is the oldest surviving house of worship in the castle compound. Study its simple sandstone interior, which holds the tomb of St. Ludmila. Walk along Jiřská and turn left onto Golden Lane.

NEIGHBORHOOD WALK | **117**

Prague Castle Picture Gallery

1 Admire the giant statues of battling titans adorning the 18th-century main gateway on Hradčanské náměstí. From here pass through the early baroque Matthias Gate to reach the ticket office in the second courtyard. The barrel-vaulted halls of the Prague Castle Picture Gallery (Obrazárna Pražského hradu), on the north side of the courtyard, hold what remains of the art collection of Emperor Rudolf II, who made Prague his capital. By his death in 1612, Rudolf had amassed one of the greatest collections in Europe. His successors moved part of his collection to Vienna, and what was left in Prague was raided by the Swedes during the Thirty Years' War, but some stunning pieces remain, including a triptych by Lucas Cranach the Elder that was originally installed in St. Vitus's Cathedral. "Young Woman at her Toilet" (1512–1515) is a transcendent piece by Titian, Rudolf's favorite artist, while the grotesque, nightmarish features of a crowd of onlookers in "The Mocking of Christ" by an anonymous 16th-century Dutch painter illustrates Rudolf's eclectic tastes.

SAVVY **TRAVELER**

Prague Castle offers several types of tickets (*www.hrad.cz*). Circuit B *($$)*, covering the Old Royal Palace, St. Vitus's Cathedral, Basilica of St. George, and Golden Lane, takes about three hours. Serious history and/or architecture fans should take Circuit A *($$$)*, covering the four sites above plus the Story of Prague Castle, Powder Tower, and Rosenberg Palace. Allow about five hours. Circuit C *($$$)* covers the Prague Castle Picture Gallery and the Treasure of St. Vitus's Cathedral. Some buildings also have individual entry tickets. The Lobkowicz Palace has its own ticket office.

Second Courtyard, Prague Castle, Prague 1 • 224 373 368 • www.hrad.cz • Tickets: Circuit C $$$; individual $ • Closed Dec. 24 • Metro: Malostranská • Tram: 22

Old Royal Palace

2 The residence of Bohemian kings up until the 16th century, and the center of royal administration under the Habsburgs, the Old Royal Palace (Starý královský palác) now houses the offices of the Czech president. The present building was started in the 12th century and added to by subsequent rulers. In the late 15th century, architect

The vast Vladislav Hall hosted events such as coronations and jousting tournaments.

Benedikt Ried cleverly merged late-Gothic and Renaissance features in a redesign for the king, Vladislav Jagiello. Ried gave the huge ceremonial **Vladislav Hall** a vaulted ceiling supported by curving ribs that continue across the ceiling in looping patterns. Upstairs is the **Chancellery,** site of the Second Defenestration. In 1618, a group of Protestant Bohemian nobles—disgruntled at the loss of privileges under the Catholic Habsburg emperor Ferdinand—threw three court officials out of the window. Back downstairs, the **Diet Hall,** where the nobility assembled, has a portrait of Habsburg empress Maria Theresa, mother of Marie-Antoinette, and a copy of the Bohemian crown jewels. The exit from the palace takes you down the early 16th-century Riders Staircase, designed by Ried to allow knights on horseback to enter Vladislav Hall for indoor jousting tournaments.

Third Courtyard, Prague Castle, Prague 1 • 224 373 368 • www.hrad.cz • Tickets: Circuit A ($$$); Circuit B ($$) • Closed Dec. 24 • Metro: Malostranská • Tram: 22

HRADČANY

In the vaulted cellars beneath the Old Royal Palace, exhibits recount the history of the castle and the people associated with it.

Story of Prague Castle

3 Housed in a Gothic cellar space, the Story of Prague Castle (Příběh Pražského hradu) exhibition uses high-tech, interactive displays and historical artifacts to tell the story of the castle from prehistoric times to the present. A series of models show the stages in the castle's development, and displays of religious objects, grave robes, weapons, and jewels tell of the daily lives of the kings, queens, saints, artists, and craftsmen who lived and worked here over the last 1,000 years. Look out for the design plans of the eminent 14th-century architect Peter Parler, which illustrate the tricks and techniques employed by castle architects, and the green glass goblets specially designed to be held by greasy fingers. Particularly chilling are the pagan tombs containing bound skeletons. Preserved just as they were found, the tombs reveal that this hilltop was an ancient sacred site before the Přemyslid dynasty chose it as their stronghold.

Third Courtyard, Prague Castle, Prague 1 • 224 373 368 • www.hrad.cz • Tickets: Circuit A ($$$); individual $ • Closed Dec. 24 • Metro: Malostranská • Tram: 22

St. Vitus's Cathedral

4 The present appearance of St. Vitus's Cathedral (Chrám sv. Víta) is mainly the work of Emperor Charles IV's favorite architect, 23-year-old Peter Parler, whose vision for a sanctuary suitable for coronations and royal shrines included vertiginous spires, flying buttresses, and towering windows. Construction began in 1344 and continued for several centuries, with great artists of every century contributing to this architectural gem.

As you enter from the west end, the third chapel on the left contains the **Alphons Mucha window,** a stained-glass rendering in art nouveau style of the lives of Slav saints Cyril and Methodius. The architectural heights of the visionary Parler are evident in the soaring chancel with its bravura flourishes such as pairs of crisscrossing ribs forming intricate nets of vaulting, and original tracery on each window. The towering **tomb of St. John of Nepomuk** (see box p. 55) behind the main altar at the eastern end, is wrought with 1.5 tons (1.4 tonnes) of silver ornament. It sanctifies a figure who dared to challenge King Wenceslas IV. Nearby, stairs lead to the **crypt,** which entombs that same monarch, as well as Charles IV.

A detail from Alphons Mucha's dramatic window in St. Vitus's Cathedral

On the south side, Parler's innovations reach their apogee in the arched dome within the **St. Wenceslas Chapel,** under which rests the highly decorated tomb of St. Wenceslas, 10th-century duke of Bohemia and Czech patron saint. Gemstone-covered walls conceal the chamber where the Bohemian crown jewels are kept under lock and key (see p. 133).

Third Courtyard, Prague Castle, Prague 1 • www.hrad .cz • 224 373 584 • Tickets: Circuit A ($$$); Circuit B ($$) • Closed Dec. 24 • Metro: Staroměstská • Tram: 22

Basilica of St. George

5 Shafts of light from tall windows pierce the ancient interior of this simple sanctuary. Despite its baroque facade, added in the 17th century, the Basilica of St. George (Bazilika sv. Jiří) is the oldest church within the castle and the resting place of early forebears of the Přemyslid dynasty. The painted wooden tomb at

The interior of the Basilica of St. George. Vratislav I's painted tomb is on the right.

the front of the nave is that of Vratislav I, founder of the original church on this site in the early 10th century. A double staircase leads up to the choir, to the right of which is St. Ludmila's chapel. Wife of Borijov I, the first Christian duke of Bohemia, mother of Vratislav 1, and grandmother of St. Wenceslas, Ludmila was murdered by her daughter-in-law in 921. Canonized soon afterward, she became the first female Bohemian saint and martyr.

Third Courtyard, Prague Castle, Prague 1 • 224 373 368 • www.hrad.cz • Tickets: Circuit A ($$$); Circuit B ($$) • Closed Dec. 24 • Metro: Malostranská • Tram: 22

Golden Lane

6 The first residents of Golden Lane (Zlatá ulička), a narrow street hugging the castle's northern fortifications, were members of Emperor Rudolf II's palace guard. During the 16th century, a vast support staff that included goldsmiths, milliners, masons, coopers, and fletchers lived cheek-by-jowl in the interconnected cottages, which remained occupied until the 1950s. At street level,

Open doors invite you to explore the houses on Golden Lane.

souvenir and gift shops now rub shoulders with re-created interiors based on some of the lane's former residents. Franz Kafka briefly had an office in **No. 22**—now a bookstore. No. 12, the **House of the Historian,** was home to film historian Josef Kazda. Old posters and film cannisters fill the narrow stairway, and you can watch early black-and-white movies of Prague in the tiny cinema.

A series of interconnected rooms running through the upper floors display armor and weapons, and a large collection of torture instruments. Casting a dark shadow, the Dalibor Tower was a prison for debtors and other troublemakers. Executions were held in the courtyard of the Supreme Burgrave's House at the far end, now occupied by the **Toy Museum** *(Jiřská 4, 224 372 294, $)*, where ancient and new toys from around the world fill two floors.

Zlatá ulička, Prague Castle, Prague 1 • 224 373 368 • www.hrad.cz • Tickets: Circuit A ($$$); Circuit B ($$) • Closed Dec. 24 • Metro: Malostranská • Tram: 22

Lobkowicz Palace
See pp. 128–129.

7

Jiřská 3, Prague Castle, Prague 1 • 233 312 925 • www.lobkowicz.cz • $$ (audioguide included) • Metro: Malostranská • Tram: 22

Hradčany Square

8 A collection of stately palaces built by the Bohemian nobility line Hradčany Square (Hradčanské náměstí). The pride of the Czech National Gallery, **Schwarzenberg Palace** (Schwarzenberský palác; *Hradčanské náměstí 2, www.ngprague.cz, 233 081 713, $, closed Mon.)* houses the gallery's collection of Bohemian baroque painting and sculpture.

The sgraffito-covered palace, dating from 1567, is Prague's finest example of a Venetian-style Renaissance building. In the courtyard, carved statues by sculptors Mattias Braun and Maximilian Brokoff guard the main entrance. These artists' flair for creating movement allows the multi-ton stone giants to all but whirl their robes around them. On the ground floor, a series of displays of models, sketches, and copies illustrate the working processes of painters and sculptors. Upstairs, a rich compendium of masterfully executed, late-Renaissance and baroque-era portraits of the powerful and the mythic includes definitive works by

GOOD **EATS**

■ **MALÝ BUDDHA**
Reasonably priced, this serene, incense-scented café serving spring rolls, jasmine tea, and gingery noodle salads is a busy local hangout. **Úvoz 46, Prague 1, 220 513 894, $**

■ **U ČERNÉHO VOLA**
At the Black Ox is a (smoke-filled) beer hall. Sausages, pickled herring, and other pub standards are also on offer. **Loretánské náměstí 1, Prague 1, 220 513 481, $**

■ **U ŠEVCE MATOUŠE**
At the Cobbler Matouš is a cozy retreat offering armchairs and grand views over Malá Strana to go with its steaks and good wine list. It is just the place for a reviving repast after an afternoon of castle explorations. **Loretánské náměstí 4, Prague 1, 220 514 536, $$**

HRADČANY

A detail from Dürer's "Feast of the Rose Garlands" in the Sternberg Palace

Flemish painter Bartholomeus Spranger and Czech masters Petr Brandl and Karel Škréta.

Next to the Archbishop's Palace (Arcibiskupský palác; *open Maundy Thursday*), across the square from the Schwarzenberg Palace, is an alleyway leading to the **Sternberg Palace** (Šternberský palác; *Hradčanské náměstí 15, www.ngprague.cz, 220 515 458, $, closed Mon.*), which houses the National Gallery's collection of European art from antiquity to the end of the baroque era. Don't miss Albrecht Dürer's celebratory "Feast of the Rose Garlands" (1506) on the ground floor in the section on German and Austrian Art 15th–18th centuries. On the second floor, look out for Peter Brueghel the Younger's version of the "Adoration of the Magi," Rembrandt van Rijn's dramatic "Scholar in his Study" (1634), and Peter Paul Rubens's large-scale "Martyrdom of St. Thomas" (1636–1638).

Hradčanské náměstí, Prague 1 • Metro: Malostranská • Tram: 22

Loreto Square

9 Two blocks uphill from Prague Castle on Loreto Square (Loretánské náměstí) is the exceptionally lush—even for Prague—baroque **Loreto** (Loreta; *Loretánské náměstí 8, Prague 1, www.loreta.cz, 233 310 510, $*), a Catholic pilgrimage site said to have been built by angels. The Loreto's richly decorous facade is the work of father-and-son team Christoph and Kilian Ignatz Dientzenhofer, begun in the 18th century. Inside, at the heart of the complex, is the earlier **Santa Casa,** or Sacred House, supposedly a reproduction of the Virgin Mary's home in Nazareth where the angel Gabriel visited her. The Santa Casa's exterior is decorated with relief scenes from the life of the Virgin, and its surprisingly plain interior by Italian architect Giovanni Orsi contains a lindenwood carving of the Virgin and Child.

The Dientzenhofers also designed the **Church of the Nativity** behind the Santa Casa. Frescoes by Václav Vavřinec Reiner enliven its ornate pink-and-gold interior. Adding to the sensory overload are a sunburst-style monstrance (the vessel that holds the host during Mass) studded with 6,222 diamonds—one of an array of rich displays in the **Treasury**—and the hourly peal of the Loreto's carillon, which plays a three-minute melody based on an old Czech hymn.

Opposite the Loreto on Loretánské náměstí, 30 half-columns adorn the 440-foot-long (134 m) facade of the **Černín Palace** (Černínský palác; not open to the public). Built in the late 17th century by the Habsburg Empire's ambassador to Venice, it is one of the largest baroque palaces in Prague. Since 1918, it has housed the Ministry of Foreign Affairs, and was the inner sanctum of the communist government.

A 17th-century miter decorated with sapphires and pearls is on display in the Loreto Treasury.

Nový Svět

10 The streets north of the Loreto, which were always outside the protective castle walls, are still a world apart. Narrow, winding,

Crowd-free Nový Svět is just a stone's throw from buzzing Prague Castle.

picturesque cobblestone lanes link historic houses and artists' workshops. From Loreto Square walk north on Černínská. On the right side of the lane, you'll pass the **Gambra** gallery *(Černínská 5)*, home and workshop of the celebrated surrealist animator and filmmaker Jan Švankmajer.

When you reach Nový Svět (New World) turn right. This romantic little lane has houses dating from the 17th and 18th centuries. The 19th-century Czech violinist Františck Ondřiček was born at **At the Golden Plough** *(No. 25)*. Emperor Rudolf II's court astronomer, Tycho Brahe, lived at **At the Golden Griffin** *(No. 1)*. Standing outside, you can imagine him studying his charts of planetary movements. From the eastern end of Nový Svět, Kanovnická leads back to Hradčany Square.

Loretánské náměstí, Prague 1 • Metro: Malostranská • Tram: 22

Lobkowicz Palace

An elegant palace within the castle houses the Princely Collections of this aristocratic Bohemian family.

Brueghel the Elder's "Haymaking" celebrates the Dutch landscape and a bountiful harvest.

Dominating the eastern end of the castle complex is the fortress-like Lobkowicz Palace (Lobkovický palác), the privately owned residence of the Lobkowicz family. The family collections, which include paintings, armor and weapons, ceramics, and musical scores, fill 22 galleries on two floors. The current Prince Lobkowicz provides the audioguide commentary, adding a personal touch to the tour. Daily lunchtime chamber concerts take place in the music salon beneath the gaze of family portraits. Begin on the second floor.

■ PORTRAITS

Members of the Lobkowicz family were major landholders and power players in Bohemian politics for at least six centuries. Their collection of paintings includes a number of family and other portraits on view in the first rooms, including, in Room B, Zdeněk Popel, chancellor to three Habsburg emperors and the first Prince Lobkowicz. Also look for the Spanish **"Infanta Margerita"** by Diego Velázquez.

■ SPECIALIST COLLECTIONS

Continue through collections of ceramics and medieval armor to the **Music Room** (Room G), which displays musical instruments and scores. Don't miss Mozart's hand-written re-orchestration of Handel's "Messiah," Ludwig van Beethoven's Third Symphony, the *Eroica*, with autographed changes, or the receipt signed by Beethoven for his stipend from the seventh Prince Lobkowicz.

■ MASTERS OF PAINTING

Room H is dedicated to Pieter Brueghel the Elder's bucolic **"Haymaking"** (1565), one of a series of panels

representing months of the year. Two rooms farther on are two large scenes of celebrations on the River Thames in London painted by Canaletto.

■ FAMILY ROOMS

On the first floor, a remarkable collection of female portraits fill the **Ernestine Room** (Room K). They were painted by the 17th century Princess Ernestine of Nassau-Siegen, whose daughter married the third Prince Lobkowicz. In the quirky **Bird Room** (Room L), illustrations of birds made with real feathers and perched on painted branches cover the walls. The tour ends with the music salon and the family chapel.

Jiřská 3, Prague Castle, Prague 1 • 233 312 925 • www.lobkowicz.cz • $$ (audioguide included) • Metro: Malostranská • Tram: 22

Royal City

The Přemyslid dynasty created strongholds at Hradčany on the west side of the Vltava and at Vyšehrad on the east bank. In the 14th century, Emperor Charles IV put his stamp on Prague with an ambitious building program that transformed whole areas of the city. Only two Habsburg emperors chose Prague as their capital, but both added a number of baroque flourishes.

The Vyšehrad promontory, site of an early Přemyslid fortress. Opposite: The two figures beneath the central panel of the Golden Gate's mosaic on St. Vitus's Cathedral represent Emperor Charles IV and his wife Elizabeth.

Founding Myths

Prophecies, palace intrigues, murders, strategic marriages, and land deals are the stuff of any long-running, royal-family story, and Bohemia's early princes certainly lived up to the narrative. According to Czech legend, the mythic warlord Kroc, whose daughter Libuše married the ploughman Přemysil (see sidebar p.144), was the first leader to establish a stronghold at **Vyšehrad.** During the late tenth century it became a stronghold of the Přemislyds. In the 11th century, Vratislav II chose it as his residence and strengthened the fortifications.

Tracing the Ruins

Few traces of the Přemislyd's original strongholds survive above ground today, but you can still make out the shapes of the earliest battlements if you know where to look. At Prague Castle, in the north passage between the first and second courtyards outside the **Spanish Hall,** you can see partially excavated walls of early battlements. More lie behind the grillework on the south side

HRADČANY

of **St. Vitus's Cathedral** (see pp. 120–122). Just across the way in the **Basilica of St. George** (see pp. 122–123) lie the tombs of Přemyslid princes Vratislav I (ruled 915–921) and Boleslav II the Pious (ruled 972–999).

Charting Bloodlines

The **Golden Gate** on the south facade of St. Vitus's features a Gothic mosaic, at the base of which are the figures of Charles IV and his fourth wife Elizabeth of Pomerania. Charles, son of John of Luxembourg, became King of Bohemia in 1346 and Holy Roman Emperor in 1355, and conveniently traced a branch of his ancestry to the Přemyslid line through his paternal grandmother. Among many of Charles's building projects that still stand is the jagged, white-stone **Hunger Wall** running

ROYAL **ROUTE**

Kings of Bohemia followed a route, known as the Royal Route, through central Prague to their coronations at Prague Castle (Pražský hrad; see pp. 118–124). Starting on Celetná in Staré Město, they processed along Karlova and across the **Charles Bridge** (Karlův most; see pp. 54–55), up **Nerudova** (see pp. 98–99), and continued west to the **Strahov Monastery** (Strahovský klášter; see pp. 104–107). Here the procession swung back east and progressed down to **Hradčany Square** (Hradčanské náměstí; see pp. 124–125) and into the castle courtyard.

HRADČANY

Charles IV's Hunger Wall was a public works project.

up Malá Strana's Petřín Hill (see p. 103), which he commissioned to provide employment to the poor. In 1348, he founded the **Charles University,** or Carolinum, one of the first and greatest universities in Central Europe. It still enlightens students today, and the original Gothic building opposite the Estates Theater in Staré Město hosts graduation ceremonies.

Leisure Class

The House of Habsburg, the dynasty that ruled the Holy Roman Empire from the 15th century onward and secured the Bohemian throne in the 16th century, could also trace their ancestry back to the Přemislyds. Most Habsburg emperors ruled from the court in Vienna, but two preferred to make Prague their capital. Ferdinand I, who became King of Bohemia in 1526 and Holy Roman Emperor in 1558, commissioned the **Royal Gardens** (see p. 134) as both a playground and a laboratory of sorts for natural sciences, a subject that fascinated all the fashionable royal retainers during this age of discovery. The garden's Queen Anne's Summer Palace was his prize project in 1538. The nearby Ball Game Court, dating from 1567, was rushed to completion so that rackets could get swinging. Today, exhibitions and concerts in the gardens carry on the spirit of escape.

Ferdinand's grandson, the iconoclastic Rudolf II (ruled 1576–1611), also based his court in Prague. He gathered around him at Hradčany some of the most colorful figures of the late Renaissance, including alchemist conmen such as Edward Kelley and John Dee, and astronomers Tycho Brahe and Johannes Kepler. Rudolf was also a patron of the arts, and what remains of his once vast art collection now fills the **Prague Castle Picture Gallery** (see p. 118).

Hidden Treasure

One area of the castle kept under strict lock and key—seven keys, in fact, distributed among the nation's top political and church leaders—is the chamber in St. Vitus's Cathedral where the Bohemian crown jewels—the Crown of St. Wenceslas, a sceptre, and orb— are kept, being taken out only on rare state occasions. According to legend, any imposter who puts on the crown will die within the year. One not-so-lucky opportunist was Nazi governor Reinhard Heydrich, who, it's said, dared try it on. A few months later the prophecy was fulfilled when a group of Czech paratroopers assassinated him.

Charles IV and subsequent kings of Bohemia wore the Crown of St. Wenceslas at their coronations.

Secret Gardens

Prague is particularly rich in green spaces—many of them surprisingly large considering the real estate values in the city center. Gardens and parks offer essential breathing spaces for relaxation and contemplation—formerly the exclusive preserve of royalty and monks, but now available to all.

■ ROYAL GARDENS

By far the most decorous of Prague's open spaces, the castle's Royal Gardens (Královská zahrada) are a former retreat for kings and consorts. At the eastern end is one of Bohemia's finest Renaissance structures, **Queen Anne's Summer Palace.** Unluckily for the queen, she was never able to enjoy it, having died before it was completed. Other features include a modernized **Orangerie** and the 16th-century **Ball Game Court.**

Mariánské hradby, Prague 1 • Metro: Malostranská • Tram: 22

■ LEDEBOURG GARDENS

Look for an unremarkable entranceway, known only to locals, on the Old Castle Steps (Staré zámecké schody) linking the castle's eastern end to Malá Strana below. Stairways link a series of terraced gardens stepping down the hillside,

finally depositing you at the rear of the Pálffy Palace (Pálffyovský palác) on Valdštejnská. The route avoids the crowds and the souvenir stands that line the usual ways down from Hradčany. Neglected during the communist era, the route has been lovingly restored—in part through the sponsorship of the U.K.'s Prince Charles.

Staré zámecké schody, Prague 1 • Metro: Malostranská • Tram: 22

■ VRTBA GARDENS

Laid out in 1720, this baroque gem in Malá Strana is overlooked by a viewing platform decorated with mythic gods sculpted by Matthias Braun. Colorful plantings and well-trimmed shrubs form complex swirling patterns in the terraced garden below.

Karmelitská 25, Prague 1 • 272 088 350 • Metro: Malostranská • Tram: 22

HRADČANY

Petřín Hill Flower Garden provides quiet and seclusion.

■ PETŘÍN HILL FLOWER GARDEN

Near the much better known Rose Garden (Růžová zahrada) beside the Observatory on Petřín Hill is the Flower Garden (Květnice). Filled with beds of perennials and bulbs, it has plenty of benches for those wanting a rest.

Karmelitská, Prague 1 ▪ Metro: Malostranská ▪ Tram: 20, 22

■ FRANCISCAN GARDEN

To escape the bustle of Nové Město's Wenceslas Square, in fine weather the locals slip off to this walled, former Franciscan monastery garden using the hidden entrance in the Světozor shopping passage on Vodičkova. The Franciscan Garden (Františkánská zahrada) offers quiet moments on mellow, shrub-lined paths, a kids' playground, and whitewashed benches that are ideal spots for reading. From 1604 until the communists threw open the gates in the 1950s, this was the monks' herb garden. Now the only reminder of their presence is the adjacent Our Lady of the Snows.

Vodičkova and Václavské náměstí, Prague 1 ▪ Metro: Můstek ▪ Tram: 3, 9, 14, 24

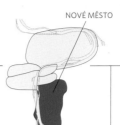

Nové Město

The name Nové Město, or New Town, and its modern, urban look belie the vision of Charles IV, Holy Roman Emperor and Bohemia's greatest king, who in 1348 decreed the layout of these few dozen blocks to the south of Staré Město. Prague's wealth and trading power during Charles's reign is evident from the large swathes of land—most notably on the sites of today's Wenceslas Square and Charles Square—that he ordered to be cleared to make way for a series of great open markets. These two extended rectangles still form the basis of the district, although the surrounding streets, parks, churches, and shops make for a diverse and dynamic commercial hub. Bounded on the west by the Vltava River, Nové Město is probably best viewed from the embankment in the late afternoon as the sun's glow hits the art nouveau facades of its riverside apartment buildings, which would not look out of place in Paris.

◐ **With swaying curves and rippling rows of windows, the Dancing House cuts a dash on Nové Město's riverfront.**

Nové Město

With wide boulevards, dignified museums, fashionable arcades, and classic parks, the city's vibrant commercial heart is all about style.

① Wenceslas Square (see p. 140) Enjoy the square's architectural gems before strolling to the National Museum at the square's southeast end.

② National Museum (see pp. 146–147) The National Museum was built to enshrine Czechoslovak identity. Check out an exhibition, then head back along the southern side of Wenceslas Square.

③ Lucerna Passage (see p. 141) This Jazz Age retail arcade features grand staircases, concert halls, and boutique shopping among other delights. Browse its glass-ceilinged halls and then turn left onto Vodičkova.

⑨ National Theater (see p. 145) End the day as Czechs do and head for the theater to enjoy a ballet, opera, or play.

⑧ Dancing House (see p. 144) Known as the "Fred and Ginger" building, this office tower combines architectural inspiration and fine dining. Hop onto tram 17 or 18 north.

OPLETALOVA

Hlavní nádraží

JINDŘIŠSKÁ

Wenceslas Square
(Václavské náměstí) ①

Můstek

NÁRODNÍ TŘÍDA

Národní třída

Lucerna Passage (Pasáž **Lucerna**) ③

MANNOVA

MOST LEGIÍ

National Theater ⓪

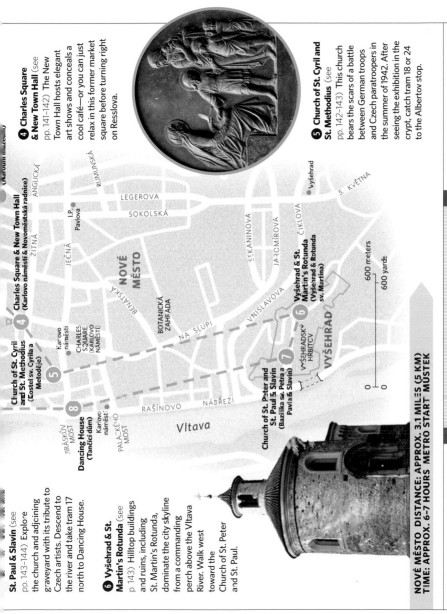

St. Paul & Slavín (see pp. 143–144) Explore the church and adjoining graveyard with its tribute to Czech artists. Descend to the river and take tram 17 north to Dancing House.

⑥ Vyšehrad & St. Martin's Rotunda (see p. 143) Hilltop buildings and ruins, including St. Martin's Rotunda, dominate the city skyline from a commanding perch above the Vltava River. Walk west toward the Church of St. Peter and St. Paul.

④ Charles Square & New Town Hall (see pp. 141–142) The New Town Hall hosts elegant art shows and conceals a cool café—or you can just relax in this former market square before turning right on Resslova.

⑤ Church of St. Cyril and St. Methodius (see pp. 142–143) This church bears the scars of a battle between German troops and Czech paratroopers in the summer of 1942. After seeing the exhibition in the crypt, catch tram 18 or 24 to the Albertov stop.

NOVÉ MĚSTO DISTANCE: APPROX. 3.1 MILES (5 KM)
TIME: APPROX. 6–7 HOURS METRO START MÚSTEK

NOVÉ MĚSTO

Wenceslas Square

1 The site of a large horse market in medieval times and the place where Czechs gathered to demand their freedom from communist domination in 1989, half-mile-long (0.5 km) Wenceslas Square (Václavské náměstí) is more of an avenue. Lined with historic and grandly decorous facades, it is the place where Prague now shows off its sense of style. Don't miss the functionalist **Bat'a** store *(No. 6)*; architect Antonín Pfeiffer and Matěj Blecha's art nouveau **Palác Koruna** *(No. 1)* featuring sculptor Vojtěch Sucharda's muscular statues around the dome; **Hotel Jalta's** showpiece 1950s' facade *(No. 45; see p. 150 for information on tours of its Cold-War-era nuclear bunker)*; and the elegant

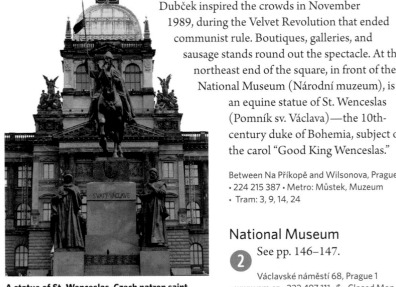

Melantrich building *(No. 36)*, constructed in 1914, from whose balcony playwright and future president Václav Havel and former party leader Alexander Dubček inspired the crowds in November 1989, during the Velvet Revolution that ended communist rule. Boutiques, galleries, and sausage stands round out the spectacle. At the northeast end of the square, in front of the National Museum (Národní muzeum), is an equine statue of St. Wenceslas (Pomník sv. Václava)—the 10th-century duke of Bohemia, subject of the carol "Good King Wenceslas."

Between Na Příkopě and Wilsonova, Prague 1 • 224 215 387 • Metro: Můstek, Muzeum • Tram: 3, 9, 14, 24

A statue of St. Wenceslas, Czech patron saint, dominates Wenceslas Square.

National Museum

2 See pp. 146–147.

Václavské náměstí 68, Prague 1 • www.nm.cz • 222 497 111 • $ • Closed Mon. • Metro: Muzeum • Tram: 11

Lucerna Passage

3 Built by Václav Havel's grandfather before World War II, this old-school retail arcade of shops, smart cafés, and vast underground concert halls and bars was once the epitome of modern city life. Today, you can catch a jazz trio or even a dance band in the space that once drew the likes of Louis Armstrong and Josephine Baker. The building is still owned by the Havel family and the arcade attracts a local clientele, who savor espresso and cakes in the cinema bar overlooking an upside-down statue of St. Wenceslas by Czech prankster artist David Černý. The many halls hide funky bookstores and other retail treats, including the **Saint Tropez** chocolate specialist and the retail store of Czech fashion designer **Ivana Follová.**

The Lucerna Passage's coffee shops draw a regular crowd.

Vodičkova 36, Prague 1 • www.lucerna.cz • Metro: Můstek • Tram: 3, 9, 14, 24

Charles Square & New Town Hall

4 Marking the northern point of Charles Square (Karlovo náměstí), the surprisingly modern looking New Town Hall (Novoměstská radnice; 224 948 229, tower $, closed Oct.–April and Mon.) was erected in the 1360s as part of Emperor Charles IV's grand plans for an expanded new town. Less than a century later, Protestant upstarts, or Hussites, led by the priest and radical Hussite representative Jan Želivský, perfected the Czech political-protest technique known as defenestration by hurling the city's corrupt Catholic mayor and his clerks from the building's austere sandstone tower. You can catch the best view of the square from the site of this act of rebellion, which Praguers still fondly recall.

At the southwest end of the square stands the baroque **Faust House** (Faustův dům), where legend has it that the devil traded riches for a soul (though not that of Dr. Faust). Today, the building offers a picturesque setting for locals taking their lunch breaks on the benches round about.

Between Žitná and U Nemocnice, Prague 2 • www.nrpraha.cz • 224 948 229 • Metro: Karlovo náměstí • Tram: 3, 6, 18, 22, 24

Church of St. Cyril and St. Methodius

5 It's easy to miss the wreaths and candles perpetually left beside the bullet-scarred side entrance to the crypt of the baroque-era Church of St. Cyril and St. Methodius (Kostel sv. Cyrila a Metoděje). They commemorate the firefight that took place on June 18, 1942, between German SS troops and seven British-trained Czech paratroopers hiding in the crypt. A month earlier, the paratroopers had assassinated Reinhard Heydrich, Nazi governor of Bohemia and Moravia. After several hours of fighting, the assassins killed themselves rather than be caught. A **memorial plaque** tells

A Czech Orthodox priest conducts a service at the Church of St. Cyril and St. Methodius.

the story, while the exhibits in the two-room **museum** in the crypt (entered from Na Zderaze) convey the chilling details of the manhunt for the men behind the highest-level coup of World War II, including the liquidation of the Czech villages of Lidice and Ležáky by the Nazis and the paratroopers' desperate last moments.

Resslova 9, Prague 2 • www.prague.net • 224 92 06 86 • $ • Closed Mon. • Metro: Karlovo náměstí • Tram: 3, 6, 18, 22, 24

Vyšehrad & St. Martin's Rotunda

6 The trek to the ruined fortress of Vyšehrad on a high promontory overlooking Prague is worth the effort for the palpable sense of past centuries that lingers among the windblown granite ruins of scattered fortifications and religious buildings. Originally, the fortress was the seat of the Přemyslid monarchs during the 10th century.

Standing out among the haunting statues within the fortress walls is the 11th-century Romanesque chapel of St. Martin (Rotunda sv. Martina). Circular in shape to afford the devil no corner to hide in, it is one of three rotundas in the city that have survived since medieval times. It is rarely open, but conveys its importance as a sacred site through a simple dignity.

V Pevnosti 5b, Prague 2 • www.praha-vysehrad.cz • 241 410 348 • Metro: Vyšehrad • Tram: 3, 7, 8, 16, 17, 24

Church of St. Peter and St. Paul & Slavín

7 The piercing 19th-century spires of the blackened sandstone Church St. Peter and St. Paul (Bazilika sv. Petra a Pavla) overlook the setting for myths about the founding of Prague

GOOD **EATS**

■ **JÁMA**
A range of excellent beers, an award-winning bacon cheeseburger, and all the Czech classics are on offer in this international-style pub. It has a quiet back patio.
V Jámě 7, 222 967 081, $

■ **NOVOMĚSTSKÝ PIVOVAR**
This underground labyrinth of classic Czech beer halls serves schnitzels, pork knee, beef in cream sauce, dumplings, and rivers of historic house beer, Novoměstské. **Vodičkova 20, 222 232 448, $$$**

■ **THE GLOBE BOOKSTORE & COFFEEHOUSE**
Mexican food, brunches, and latte accompany book readings and screenings of movies and sports events. **Pštrossova 6, 224 934 203, $$**

NOVÉ MĚSTO

IN **THE KNOW**

Some of the best-known Slav myths chronicle the life of Libuše, a warrior princess said to have lived on the hilltop where Vyšehrad now stands. Like many European nations, Czechs hold dear a founding myth involving a farmer. One version has Libuše transfixed by a vision of a great city that would arise from her union with a farmer, and she chooses a plowman called Přemysl with whom to settle down and found the dynasty that would build a Golden City. You can see Libuše's image and that of Přemysl with his horse and plow on official seals and Prague municipal buildings to this day.

(see sidebar left). The church began as an 11th-century chapel and was expanded later into its current neo-Gothic form. Architect Josef Mocker added the elaborate rose window and soaring towers during reconstruction in 1885–1903. The haunting relief carving of **The Last Judgment** by sculptor Štěpán Zálešák over the main door was added at the same time.

In the cemetery next to the church you see a large, ornate tomb known as the **Slavín.** This densely packed resting place houses the individual tombs of about 55 renowned Czech artists, composers, and literati, including Prague-born artist Alphons Mucha and 19th-century composers Antonín Dvořák and Bedřich Smetana.

V Pevnosti 5b, Prague 2 • www.praha-vysehrad.cz • 241 410 348 • Church of St. Peter and St. Paul: $ • Metro: Vyšehrad • Tram: 3, 7, 8, 16, 17, 24

Dancing House

8 Seeming to sway like movie stars in the middle of a ballroom number, the Dancing House (Tančící dům) has the nickname "Fred and Ginger" building for good reason. This ambitious architectural project, the creation of Czech-Croatian architect Vlado Milunić and Canadian-born Frank Gehry, occupies a historic riverside site and was completed in 1996 with backing from Václav Havel, who grew up in the next-door building. Offices fill most floors, but at the top you can find the **Céleste Restaurant** (*www.celeste restaurant.cz, 221 984 160, $$$$–$$$$$*), which combines upscale dining with extensive views of Prague.

Intersection of Rašínovo and Resslova, Prague 2 • Metro: Karlovo náměstí • Tram: 14, 17

NOVÉ MĚSTO

National Theater

9 Czech patriots, with their passion for *divadlo*, as theater is known, were so dedicated to this building (Národní divadlo) that they twice raised the money for its construction. The original theater opened in 1881 but burned down shortly afterward. Within two years a replacement went up, with improvements such as newfangled electric lighting and steel beams. The auditorium hosts modern and classic opera, plays, and ballet. Book a balcony seat if you want to soak up the atmosphere in this chandeliered, Renaissance-revival space adorned with ceiling frescoes and curvacious box railings. If you prefer something more contemporary, the theater's New Stage in the blocky glass tower next door puts on dance, drama, and Laterna magika productions, which combine dance and visual effects.

Národní 2, Prague 1 • www.narodni-divadlo.cz • 224 901 448 • $–$$$$$ • Metro: Můstek, Národní Třída • Tram: 6, 9, 17, 18, 22

A production of Antonín Dvořák's *The Jacobin* at the National Theater

National Museum

National collections covering prehistory, Czech history, and natural history reside in this grand building and its neighbor.

The National Museum's entrance hall hosts regular concerts—a good way to enjoy the opulent interior.

Designed to convey a glorious past and a nascent Bohemian identity, the National Museum (Národní muzeum) was always intended as far more than a repository for mammoths and marble busts. Joseph Mocker's mid-19th-century building epitomized the monumental style of the Czech National Revival movement at that time. In contrast to the main building's imposing neo-Renaissance facade of columns, arches, and allegorical figures, the glassy, modernist National Museum New Building next door dates from 1930.

■ HALLS AND HEROES

The interior of the 19th-century National Museum is a main attraction in itself; its first-floor atrium is a real showstopper. Ornate staircases crisscross each other in front of three floors of faux-marble walls, balustrades, and walkways, all in the shifting natural glow of skylit space under a fabulous glass dome. Busts of national heroes from the worlds of diplomacy, science, and the arts fill out the imperious space but can hardly compete with it. Climb the dome for a breathtaking view of Staré Město and Prague Castle.

■ LIVING HISTORY

The National Museum's collections run to several million items drawn from natural history, paleontology, anthropology, archaeology, and minerals. Some of its most prized items date from classical Greek and Roman times and others illustrate the development and culture of the Czechoslovak people from prehistory to the present day. The newly reorganized displays show items from across the collections in five integrated major exhibits. The renovated second floor also features an interactive

IN THE KNOW

Several years of renovation work on the National Museum's main building are greatly increasing the space available for the museum's collections. The permanent collections are being reorganized and displayed in both buildings, and the main building's two courtyards will have new glass roofs, providing more space for temporary exhibitions. An underground passage will connect the two buildings.

learning center designed to appeal to kids and students.

■ MODERN ADDITION

The lower floors of the modernist, gray-tinted, stone-and-glass New Building originally housed the Prague Stock Exchange. The upper floors, supported on concrete pillars, were added during the communist era. After the Velvet Revolution, the building housed the Radio Free Europe offices before becoming the boldest and newest addition to Prague's multi-venue National Museum. It mounts temporary exhibitions on a variety of themes, such as the history of money and the Czech role in World War I.

NOVÉ MĚSTO

Václavské náměstí 68, Prague 1 • www.nm.cz • 222 497 111 • The main building is due to reopen in 2015, but check the website for the latest information • $ • Metro: Muzeum • Tram: 11

Soviet Legacy

In summer 1945, the Red Army negotiated the right to liberate Prague after exaggerating its progress to General Eisenhower, the Allied commander in Europe. Meanwhile, 1,500 Czechs died in an uprising against the German occupiers. The deception worked: Once installed in Prague, the Soviets held power until 1989. Signs of the regime remain throughout the city, fading a little more each year.

NOVÉ MĚSTO

The Memorial to the Victims of Communism at the base of Petřín Hill. Opposite: A sunken cross marks the spot where Jan Palach set himself alight on Wenceslas Square.

A Void on the Square

The curiously jagged northern face of **Old Town Hall** (Staroměstská radnice; see p. 63) in Staré Město marks the place where, in May 1945, German artillery and fire bombs destroyed its centuries-old administration building. During the uprising, resistance fighters had hidden stolen weapons in the cellar—where you can still spot burned beams from the clashes.

All over the city center, small bronze plaques consisting of a sculpted hand with first two fingers raised mark places where resistance fighters died. Buildings around Old Town Square and **Wenceslas Square** (see p. 140), which at the time were filled with makeshift barricades, feature dozens of the darkened reminders.

More Than a Museum

The National Museum's commanding position at the top of Wenceslas Square has put it in the line of fire more than once. Until its renovation, it bore scars from machine-gun and rifle fire sustained during the 1968 Warsaw Pact invasion. Moscow had ordered tanks into the city to quash the spreading liberalization, free speech, and other civic reforms of the Prague Spring allowed under communist First Secretary Alexander Dubček.

Torch No. 1

The pedestrian area around the equine statue of St. Wenceslas at the top of the eponymously named square features a sidewalk memorial at the spot where, on January 16, 1969, Charles University student Jan Palach set himself alight to protest at the Soviet-led occupation in 1968 that had dashed all hopes of reform. He left a note signed "Torch No. 1," throwing the government into a frenzy of investigations in an attempt to gain control of what they believed would be a

VODKA **POWER**

Prague's most tongue-in-cheek tribute to the bad old days is the **Propaganda** bar, owned and operated by the proprietor of the Museum of Communism. The bar's decor seemingly employs all the pieces that couldn't fit into the museum. The vodkas are appropriately inflammatory. **Michalská 12, Prague 1, www.propagandapub.cz**

mass movement of protest suicides. In the end, just two more young people followed in Palach's footsteps: Jan Zajíc and Evžen Plocek.

No Angels

One of the trade-offs of the return to what the Soviets called Normalization after they forced Dubček out was the Prague Metro, built in the 1970s. Stations in Moscow were named for Prague, and the Prague B line station now called **Anděl** (Angel) was then known as Moskevská. A communist-era frieze over one escalator entrance still features the name, making the station a popular movie backdrop.

Underground Movement

Wenceslas Square bears a particular concentration of marks of passing regimes. **Hotel Jalta** (*Václavské náměstí 15, www.jalta.cz*), built in the 1950s, recently opened a series of Cold War bunkers buried deep beneath its lobby. The staff is happy to take visitors on a guided tour of the secret radio room, makeshift operating theater, and submarine-like living quarters for a handful of party elite—the only people who knew of the existence of this strategic nuclear-war shelter with its convincing cover as a prime downtown hotel.

The Žižkov district's hillside Parukářka Park also hides an extensive network of tunnels and bunkers dating back to the 1950s. These days, the concrete, graffiti-covered bunker walls on Prokopova conceal a bar—the **Parukářka bunkr**—a climbing wall, a collection of communist-era military uniforms and gas masks, and a company offering tours of the once top-secret hideout (*www.parukarka.eu*). You might even catch an indie rock show—if you can find the entrance behind the steel blast-door at the western end of Prokopova.

Ghostly Memorial

Reached via the steep paths leading up Vítkov (Žižkov) Hill from the Tachovské náměstí tram stop on Husitská, this promontory just north of Parukářka is Prague's most visible reminder of the bad old days of communism. Built in the 1920s to honor the Czech Legionnaires, who fought against the Habsburgs in World War I, and guarded by an equine statue of the 15th-century Hussite leader, Jan Žižka, the **National Memorial** (Národní památník; *U Památníku 1900, www.nm.cz, 222 781 676, closed Mon.–Tues., $*) became a mausoleum for three communist-era presidents. Their remains have since been removed, and the building now houses an exhibition on the history of Czechoslovakia in the 20th century.

Marking the March

Students led the mass demonstrations that finally pushed out the Czech communist regime in November 1989. A bronze memorial marks the spot at **Národní, No. 16,** in Nové Město, where some of the 10,000 protesters confronted riot police on November 17, International Students' Day. On December 18, 2011, candles and flowers covered the memorial following the death of former president, Václav Havel.

Counting Costs

Across the Vltava River in Malá Strana, the **Memorial to the Victims of Communism** (Pomník obětem komunismu; *Újezd and Vítězná*) is a tribute created in 2002 by sculptor Olbram Zoubek and architects Jan Kerel and Zdeněk Hölzl. A series of hollow, broken, naked bronze figures descend Petřín Hill alongside a strip of metal that catalogs the 205,486 people arrested, the 170,938 forced into exile, the 4,500 who died in prison, and 575 others who met violent ends at state hands between 1948 and 1989.

The public creates a tribute to Václav Havel in Wenceslas Square following his death.

City Views

Surrounded by hills and packed with high-reaching towers and spires, Prague spoils visitors with its wealth of views. Hilltop gardens offer sweeping panoramas; spires and towers provide these, too, as well as up-close views of the many statues and ornaments that decorate buildings at roof level.

NOVÉ MĚSTO

■ ANCIENT VANTAGE

To feel the frisson of the warring progenitors of Czech dynasties, direct your hiking boots toward the hilltop ruins of **Vyšehrad** (see p. 143). Here, just a 13-minute tram ride from downtown Prague, your view overlooks the Vltava River to the west, with the city lying at your feet to the north. In afternoon light, the 11th-century St. Martin's Rotunda, cemetery headstones of cultural heroes, and Přemyslid castle battlements glow with a sense of history.

■ OVERLOOKING THE OLD CENTER

From the top of **Old Town Hall tower** (see p. 63), Staré Město's roof gables look close enough to touch. The 360-degree view takes in the Žižkov TV Tower to the southeast and the National Museum on Wenceslas Square to the south, the Strahov Monastery to the west, and the wooded hills of Letná Park to the north. Relatively few visitors make it to the top of the Old Town Hall tower, but to really have the city skyline to yourself, try the even less visited **Kotva** department store roof terrace (*Náměstí Republiky 8, Prague 1, 224 801 111*), known only to locals.

■ LEFT-BANK PROSPECTS

Industrial-Age Bohemia lives on in Malá Strana, where the Observation Tower (see p. 103) on **Petřín Hill** offers a thrilling 299-step climb to two viewing platforms, where you can feel the sway on windy days. Keeping your back to the communist-era suburbs to the west, you can pick out key landmarks such as the Church of St. Nicholas among the surrounding spires and, on the far bank of the river, the National Theater and beyond that the National Memorial on Vítkov Hill. At 295 feet (90 m) high, the tower of

The Hanavský Pavilion's terrace provides a great view of Prague's succession of bridges.

St. Vitus's Cathedral (see pp. 120–122) offers a bird's-eye view of Prague Castle with the city stretching away in every direction— not to mention a close encounter with the cathedral's gargoyles.

■ VIEW FROM THE TERRACE
Nowhere in Prague beats the iron, glass, and brick **Hanavský Pavilion** (see p. 158) in Holešovice's Letná Park for a view of the bridges over the Vltava River, six of which line up as you gaze south. This spot is ideal for a twilight Pilsner as the lights on the Charles Bridge begin to glow. The city's surfeit of expert film crews ensure plenty of dramatic illumination, whether the subject is the undersides of ancient arches, Prague Castle, or the spires of the Týn Church on Old Town Square.

■ CITY ON THE HILL
Arguably the finest view of Prague Castle is from the hilltop **National Memorial** (see p. 151) at Vítkov in the Žižkov district. Looking west from the base of General Jan Žižka's equestrian statue, the whole city is laid out below, with the distant castle clustered around the towers of St. Vitus's Cathedral.

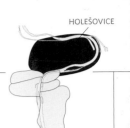

Holešovice

Locals have always cherished the views of Prague's historic center from Holešovice's Letná Park; and this increasingly trendy district is now attracting visitors, too. Embraced by a bend in the Vltava River to the north of Josefov, this area of former industrial buildings and a railyard hub has undergone many changes. The neo-baroque Hanavský Pavilion in Letná Park—a survivor of the 1891 World Fair—now stands where Bronze Age tribes once kept guard. The Veletržní Palace, which in the 1920s housed trade fairs exhibiting the newest consumer fads, hosts the National Gallery's collection of modern and contemporary art. Today's trade fairs launch at the Exhibition Grounds, which are also home to the Prague Planetarium, established in 1935, and the Lapidárium's large collection of statuary. And the district's plethora of disused factory buildings are fast being adapted to show off the latest trends in art and design.

◐ A 164-foot-high (50 m) wrought-iron clock tower adorns the Exhibition Grounds' Industrial Palace.

Holešovice

Positioned on the fringe of Prague's historic center, the district has a mix of hands-on museums, cutting-edge galleries, and large parks.

6 U Průhonu (see p. 161) Wander this and the neighboring streets for a variety of small shops and galleries housed in former industrial buildings.

HOLEŠOVICE

STROMOVKA PARK
(KRÁLOVSKÁ OBORA
STROMOVKA)

Exhibition Grounds
(Výstaviště) **4**

POD KAŠTANY

KORUNOVAČNÍ

Veletržní Palace
(Veletržní palác)

VELETRŽNÍ

National
Technical Museum
(Národní technické muzeum) **2**

Hradčanská

BADENIHO

Letná Park **1**
(Letenské sady)

LETENSKÝ
TUNEL

ŠTEFÁNIKŮV
MOST

NÁBŘEŽÍ KAPIT

NÁBŘEŽÍ EDVARDA BENEŠE

DVOŘÁKOVO NÁBŘEŽÍ

1 Letná Park (see p. 158) This hilltop park features two retro expo pavilions, modern sculpture, and the finest views of Staré Město in the district. Leave the park at the eastern end and head for Kostelní.

2 National Technical Museum (see pp. 158–159) Explore this compendium of Czechnology collections, which include classic cars and planes and a crafty exhibit on spying and encryption tools. Head east on Kostelní and turn north on Dukelských Hrdinů.

HOLEŠOVICE   DISTANCE: 2.8 MILES (4.5 KM)
TIME: APPROX. 8 HOURS   METRO START: HRADČANSKÁ

⑤ DOX Center for Contemporary Art

(see p. 161) This newest addition to the gallery scene typifies Holešovice's rising tide of art and design. Examine work from Prague's most daring and innovative painters, sculptors, and multimedia mavens. Walk south on Osadní and turn left on U Průhonu.

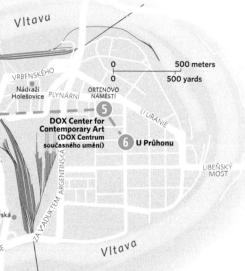

④ Exhibition Grounds (see pp. 159-160)

A planetarium and the National Museum's sculpture collection are two of the attractions at this historic trade fair site. Head northeast on U Výstaviště and continue on Partyzánská. Turn east onto Na zátorách and continue on Plynární. Turn south onto Osadní and then east onto Poupětova. Alternatively, take tram 12 to the Ortenovo náměstí stop.

③ Veletržní Palace

(see pp. 162-163) The Czech Republic's prime showcase for its modern and contemporary art collections, this former trade show hall hosts a rich array of Czech and international work. Walk north on Dukelských Hrdinů.

HOLEŠOVICE

Historic planes, cars, and motorbikes fill the National Technical Museum's main hall.

Letná Park

1 The city's most visible green space, Letná Park (Letenské sady) hosts several attractions. The metal-domed **Hanavský Pavilion** at the western end was built for the 1891 Jubilee World Fair. Its patio restaurant offers snacks and meals to go with the amazing view. Artist Vratislav Novák's giant **metronome sculpture** at the meeting point of the footpaths leading up from the river occupies a spot vacated when, in 1960, the finest Czech pyrotechnicians were ordered to blow up a ten-story-high statue of Stalin that stood here.

Letenské sady, Prague 7 • 233 378 208 • Metro: Hradcanská • Tram: 1, 8, 12, 25, 26

National Technical Museum

2 Among the dozens of rivals in a city seemingly obsessed with museums, none can match the thrills of the National Technical Museum (Národní technické muzeum). Twelve permanent exhibits cover themes such as Transportation, Astronomy, Measurement of Time, and Chemistry Around Us. Stars of the transportation section include historic aircraft, antique Laurin & Klement touring cars, Jawa motorbikes, fighter planes, and steam locomotives. The cosmic wonders displays are a hit with the younger generation. You can play with color perception and motion capture in the Space, Color, and Movement (Prostor, barva, a pohyb) display or try out your spying skills in the interactive Top Secret exhibit.

Kostelní 42, Prague 7 • 220 399 111 • www.ntm.cz • $ • Closed Mon. • Metro: Hradčanská • Tram: 1, 8, 12, 25, 26

Veletržní Palace

3 See pp. 162–163.

Dukelských hrdinů 47, Prague 7 • www.ntm.cz • 224 301 122 • $ • Closed Mon. • Metro: Nádraží Holešovice • Tram: 12, 17, 24

Exhibition Grounds

4 With a vast wrought-iron and stained-glass central arch supporting a winding iron staircase that leads up to a whimsical cupola clock, Bedřich Münzberger's art nouveau style **Industrial Palace** (Průmyslový palác) from the 1891 Jubilee World Fair provides a spectacular welcome to Prague's Exhibition Grounds (Výstaviště). The building is still used for trade fairs and exhibitions.

Situated among the trees and meadows to the left of the Exhibition Grounds, **Prague Planetarium** (Planetárium Praha; *Královská obora 233, www.planetarium.cz, 220 999 001, $*) is one of Výstaviště's most enchanting attractions. Programs, some of which provide an English translation, include a look at Emperor Rudolph II's obsession with astrology and alchemy, offering a

GOOD **EATS**

■ **BOHEMIA BAGEL**
Expat Glen Spicker launched the city's first proper bagel shops during the 1990s, offering bottomless coffee, all-day breakfast, and full weekend brunch. **Dukelských Hrdinů 48, 220 806 541, $**

■ **KAVÁRNA POD LIPAMI**
The Coffeehouse under the Lindens is a tribute to the classic Bohemian cafés of old. Locals gather here to read the newspapers and chat over fine espresso and homemade Sacher torte. **Čechova 1, 777 568 658, $**

■ **LETENSKÝ ZÁMEČEK**
Dine on Mediterranean fare and sip dry white wine in the courtyard or join the crowd on the river side of the path for falafels and Gambrinus beer. **Letenské sady 341, 233 378 208, $$**

HOLEŠOVICE

A young space enthusiast tries driving a Moon buggy simulator at the Planetarium.

unique, Prague-centric view of cosmic questions. In the circular theater, shows illustrating the night sky use laser effects to jazz up demonstrations of the movements of planets and constellations.

To the right of the main gates is the art nouveau **Lapidárium** (*Výstaviště 422, www.nm.cz, 233 375 636, $, closed Mon.–Tues.*), where the National Museum displays sculptures and monuments, most of them carved in stone, from around the city that are at risk of damage from the weather, pollution, or demolition. Items in the collection date from medieval times to the 19th century. Look out for the Renaissance Krocín fountain in Room 3, a large, ornate, red-marble structure that was originally in Old Town Square (Staroměstské náměstí; see p. 63). Room 6 has a number of original statues from the Charles Bridge (Karlův most; see pp. 54–55).

Areál Výstaviště 67, Prague 7 • 220 103 111 • www.incheba.cz • $ • Metro: Nádraží Holešovice • Tram: 12, 24

DOX Center for Contemporary Art

5 The city's newest significant establishment for contemporary art, the minimalist DOX Center (DOX Centrum současného umění) is leading the vanguard in reasserting Prague's claim to edgy culture. Since 2008, DOX has embraced emerging artists working in the fields of photography, video, pixelated paintings, design, and architecture. Exhibits such as "Poster: Mass Media or Art?" challenge received ideas about art and design. With accompanying talks and concerts, this is the place to catch up with 21st-century bohemians.

Exhibits at DOX challenge conventional ideas about art.

Poupětova 1, Prague 7 • 295 568 123 • www.dox.cz • Closed Tues. • Metro: Nádraží Holešovice • Tram: 12, 24

U Průhonu

6 A cluster of small shops and galleries, an art center, restaurants, and clubs pack into this block-sized area bounded by U Průhonu, Komunardů, Dělnická, and Osadní. The **Pivní Galerie** (Beer Gallery; *U Průhonu 9, Prague 7, www.pivnigalerie .cz, 220 870 613, closed Sat.–Mon.*) stocks around 150 varieties of Bohemian and Moravian beers—you can taste and buy its wares. In a former ham factory on Osadní, **Křehký Gallery** (*Osadní 35, Prague 7, www.krehky.com, 267 990 545, closed Sat.–Sun.*) shows contemporary glass and furniture by Czech and foreign designers and sells limited editions of some of the pieces on view. One block east is **La Fabrika** (*Komunardů 30, Prague 7, http://goout.cz, 604 104 600, advance reservations recommended*), where industrial history and contemporary art collide. This multipurpose arts venue in a series of former factory buildings is the place to catch a cutting-edge dance or theater performance.

U Průhonu and Komunardů, Prague 7 • Metro: Nádraží Holešovice • Tram: 1, 3, 5, 25

HOLEŠOVICE

Veletržní Palace

The former Trade Fair Palace is a fitting home for the nation's greatest collection of modern and contemporary art.

Four floors of galleries surround the Veletržní Palace's vast atrium.

Since 1995, this glass-and-concrete sanctuary has housed the National Gallery's collection of modern art, which ranges from French Impressionism to contemporary installations. Paintings by Alphons Mucha and other visionary Czech painters, and those of their mentors, including Henri Matisse, Amedeo Modigliani, and the young Picasso, are on show. The gallery also celebrates Prague's post-World War II generation of artists, whose work could not be widely seen at the time. Begin on the ground floor and work your way up.

HOLEŠOVICE

■ MUCHA COMES HOME

When Alfons Mucha's **Slav Epic** (*Slovanská epopej*), a cycle of 20 vast paintings, went on show in the main hall in 2012, it was their first appearance in Prague in 80 years. Painted between 1912 and 1926, these massive canvasses—the largest measures 18 x 24 feet (6 x 8 m)—portray scenes from Slav mythology. "Cycle No. 14: The Defence of Sziget by Nikola Zrinski" in particular epitomizes Mucha's unrestrained theatricality.

■ INTERNATIONAL COUPS

International influences, especially from Vienna and Paris, have strongly influenced Czech art. Work on the first floor presents a survey of these founts of inspiration, including Gustav Klimt, Oskar Kokoschka, Edvard Munch, and Joan Miró.

■ MODERNISM CZECH-STYLE

The second floor is the place to catch the pulse of Prague's 20th-century art scene. The emergence of Czech abstract art was led by František Kupka, whose painting *"Amorpha, Fugue en deux couleurs"* illustrates his obsession with the harmonics of contrasting color bands. Look for

IN **THE KNOW**

When architects Oldřich Tyl and Josef Fuchs designed the Trade Fair Palace in the 1920s, they had the space to be bold. They produced a Manhattan-influenced, functionalist building filled with natural light thanks to the rectangular structure with six floors of balconies around a glass-roofed, canyon-like atrium. Destroyed by fire, it was rebuilt and opened as the jewel in the National Gallery's crown in 1995.

the collage work of the influential Jiří Kolář, the pioneering, computer-assisted abstract art of Zdeněk Sýkora, and painter Rudolf Fila's reinterpretations of Gustav Klimt.

■ FRENCH INFLUENCE

Move up to the third floor for the Impressionists and Postimpressionists, from Claude Monet to Vincent van Gogh and Paul Gauguin, whose paintings sit seamlessly alongside the surrealist work of painter Jan Zrzavý and other early Czech boundary breakers. Especially good are the cubist paintings and sculpture of Otto Gutfreund and the streamlined bronze racer in Otakar Švec's 1924 **"Sunbeam Motorcycle."**

Dukelských hrdinů 47, Prague 7 • www.ntm.cz • 224 301 122 • $ • Closed Mon. • Metro: Nádraží Holešovice • Tram: 12, 17, 24

Beer Culture

Ever since Josef Groll brewed the first Pilsner-style lager in the town of Plzeň in 1842, the Czech Republic's fondness for beer, and its quality, has remained unparalleled. While bottom-fermented, pale lagers, such as Groll brewed, still reign, the Prague beer scene is evolving to include stouts and wheat beers. And small breweries, some operating in centuries-old brewery buildings, thrive.

Beer-drinking is a central part of Prague life. Opposite: Lokál is one of the city's best-known pubs.

Bohemian Brew

While Czech beer as we know it today dates from the mid-1800s, the first record of a brewery in the Czech lands was reported in 993 at Prague's Břevnov monastery. The monastery stopped producing beer in 1899, but since 2011 the microbrewery Břevnovský Pivovar (see sidebar opposite) has occupied the brewery building, producing traditional lagers alongside pale ales and a Russian Imperial Stout.

Pilsner Revolution

The lager that Groll produced for the Plzeňský Prazdroj brewery in 1842 was so popular that it sparked a revolution around the world. A bottom-fermented beer, it was golden in color and had a delicate flavor, unlike the dark, sweet beers that were commonly available at the time. Locally grown hops and pure Czech water both contribute to Pilsner lager's taste and today foreign brewers go to great lengths to replicate the specific flavors of these ingredients.

Beer on the Menu

It's not hard to find a *pivo* (beer): Nearly every restaurant, bar, and café serves one of the big three—Pilsner Urquell, Staropramen, Gambrinus—on draft. Draft beers typically come in two sizes—0.3 liters and 0.5 liters.

Lager beers, which range from light to dark in color, are the most popular style, but Czech tastes are changing, with dark, stout-style beers and top-fermented wheat beers becoming more popular, while the microbrewery scene is burgeoning. Three beers from smaller breweries to try are Únětické, Svijany, and Primator, which the World Beer Awards named world's best beer in 2013. Among the younger set, fruit beers—flavored with lemon, grapefruit, or even orange and ginger—are gaining popularity.

PRAGUE **PUBS**

Břevnovský Try the dark Břevnovský Benedict or a classic Imperial Pilsner. **Markétská 1, 220 406 294**

Lokál Serving some of the best Pilsner Urquell in the city, this is an old-school Czech pub experience. **Dlouhá 33, 222 316 265**

Pivovarský Klub This beer club serves Czech light, amber, and dark beers on tap. Try the home-brewed Štěpán beer. **Křižíkova 17, 222 315 777**

Zlý časy Beer fanatics will enjoy choosing from nearly 50 draft beers. Try one of their strong Kocours. **Čestmírova 5, 723 339 995**

HOLEŠOVICE

Small Modern Art Galleries

Prague is recognized as a world center of modern art and design, from the art nouveau movement of the early 20th century through to the currently burgeoning contemporary art scene. Rather than occurring together in art hot spots, new galleries regularly spring up across the city.

HOLEŠOVICE

■ THE CHEMISTRY GALLERY

For a glimpse at what's hot in young Czech contemporary art, head to Holešovice's The Chemistry Gallery. Anything goes here, with graffiti artists, multimedia specialists, graphics, installations . . . it's an intriguing way to see what's moving young artists today. Curators are not concerned with the medium but with building up a portfolio of artists to promote. For the visitor, it means something radically different from what is on offer in other Prague galleries.

Bubenská 1, Prague 7 • www.thechemistry.cz • 606 649 170 • Closed Mon.–Tues. • Metro: Vltavská • Tram: 3, 26

■ COLLOREDO-MANSFELD PALACE

This former baroque palace beside the Charles Bridge in Staré Město is one of City Gallery Prague's newest venues and still very much a work in progress. Changing exhibitions of contemporary art take place on the top floor. Previous shows have included Tadeáš Podracký's installation "Habitus" reflecting on the connection between art and design, and Daniel Hanzlík's environmentally themed digital video and audio installations. On the way back downstairs, on the second floor, you can take a detour through a succession of reception rooms whose 18th-century, rococo-style interiors have been preserved.

Karlova 2, Prague 1 • 222 232 053 • $ • Closed Mon., Jan. 1, Dec 24–25 • Metro: Staroměstská

■ DVORAK SEC GALLERY

Located off Staré Město's Old Town Square, Dvorak Sec mainly showcases young artists from the Czech Republic, Germany, Britain, and the United States. Exhibits range from simple paintings and sketches to monumental sculptures and light installations. Sculptor David

Dvorak Sec Gallery draws a crowd to its contemporary art shows.

Černý, one of the Czech Republic's best known artists, has held shows here, as has street art–inspired Czech painter Jakub Matuška and German new-media artist Michael Najjar.

Dlouhá 5, Praha 1 • www.dvoraksec.com • 607 262 617 • Closed Sun., public holidays • Metro: Staroměstská

■ Kampa Museum

Meda and Jan Mládek, the Czech-American partnership behind this museum on Kampa Island in Malá Strana, began promoting underground art from Central and Eastern Europe in the 1960s. The permanent exhibitions include a collection of Central European modern art; work by painter František Kupka ranging from paintings from the 1890s and turn-of-the-century sketches through to expressive abstract figure drawings; and work by sculptor Otto Gutfreund, including pieces from his cubist period. Regular temporary exhibitions feature avant-garde Czech and foreign artists.

U Sovových mlýnů 2, Prague 1 • www.museum kampa.com • 257 286 147 • $ • Closed Jan. 1, Dec. 24–25 • Tram 9, 10, 12, 16, 20, 22

The Bílkova Vila displays František Bílek's moving wood-carved sculptures.

■ MUSEUM MONTANELLI

Temporary exhibitions at this private museum in Malá Strana include work by Czech and foreign artists, as well as pieces from the DrAK Foundation, which runs the museum. Previously featured artists include Czech photographer Běla Kolářová, Chinese multimedia artist Xu Zhen, and Icelandic artist Sigrún Ólafsdóttir, whose paintings and sculpture are known for their balance and movement.

Nerudova 13, Prague 1 • www.muzeummontanelli .com • 257 531 220 • $ • Closed Mon., Jan. 1, Dec. 24–25 • Metro: Malostranská • Tram: 12, 20, 22

■ BÍLKOVA VILA

The art nouveau symbolist sculptor František Bílek designed and built this villa in Hradčany in 1910. Its features reveal a range of inspirations, from the Egyptian-style columns outside the building to the bird and leaf motifs on the metal door handles inside. The curving walls never reach a right angle and some staircases lead nowhere. The villa doubled as a studio, and examples of Bílek's work are on display, including "The Deadly Fall," carved from an uprooted oak, and bronze portraits of his children. Bílek is known for Christian themes, which he often explored through multifigure scenes from the life of Christ carved in wood.

Mickiewiczova 1, Prague 6 • 233 323 631 • $ • Closed Mon., Jan. 1, Dec. 24–25 • Metro: Hradčanská • Tram: 22

■ Mucha Museum
The Czech artist Alphons Mucha is well-known for his art nouveau advertisements and posters for Paris theaters, but this museum in Nové Město's Kaunický Palace displays examples of all his work, including paintings, sculptures, photographs, charcoal drawings, and lithographs, as well as personal memorabilia. Mucha's Paris work is particularly well represented and includes his Paris sketchbooks and a set of posters that he designed for actress Sarah Bernhardt.

Panská 7, Prague 1 • www.mucha.cz • 224 216 415 • $$ • Closed Jan. 1, Dec. 24–25 • Metro: Můstek • Tram: 3, 9

■ Galerie Václava Špály
In this gallery near Nové Město's Wenceslas Square, temporary shows focus on painting, sculpture, and photography by living Czech artists. Past shows have featured paintings by Jiří Černický, Kateřina Vincourová's sculptures, and work by leading Czech postmodernist artist Jiří David, whose hybrid style combines painting, performance, and photography.

Národní 30, Prague 1 • www.spalovka.cz • $ • Closed Jan. 1, Dec. 24–25 • Metro: Můstek

■ Leica Gallery Prague
The work of top international and Czech photographers fill this museum on the edge of Nové Město. Past shows include the work of American Elliott Erwitt, Czech-American Antonín Kratochvíl, Germans Wim and Donata Wenders, and Swiss Michel Comte.

Školská 28, Prague 1 • www.lgp.cz • 222 211 567 • $ • Closed Jan. 1, Dec. 24–25 • Metro: Můstek • Tram: 3, 9

A detail from one of Alphons Mucha's series of Byzantine heads on show in the Mucha Museum

PART 3

Travel Essentials

PLANNING YOUR TRIP

When to Go

Prague is a year-round destination, but late spring and late summer are perhaps the best times to visit. In May, June, and September, the climate is generally warm, occasionally hot, and perfect for taking advantage of the summer terraces of cafés and restaurants. If you enjoy music and the performing arts, consider coming during the Prague Spring Music Festival in the second half of May, though you will need to reserve well in advance.

There are some drawbacks to visiting Prague in high summer. It is a small city that quickly becomes crowded, especially with German and Austrian visitors, for whom it is a short hop over the border. In summer, you will need to plan your stay well in advance, securing hotel reservations as early as possible. Top or fashionable restaurants should also be booked ahead.

The summer heat can be tiring, and there are often heavy afternoon downpours in July and August.

The great advantage of visiting Prague out of season is that there are fewer tourists around. You can also benefit from low-season hotel rates, which in general apply from November through March. Winter is also the best time for cultural events. The city's main concert halls and opera houses operate year-round, but their principal seasons are fall and winter.

The biggest drawbacks of coming to Prague out of season are the cold temperatures and short days, which limit the time available for sightseeing.

Christmas in Prague can be great fun, with open-air markets, clowns, and entertainers in the streets, and the possibility of crunchy snow underfoot providing a festive flavor. On the other hand, the city can be as crowded as it is in the summer. Many hotels charge their highest rates over Christmas and New Year.

Climate

Prague enjoys a relatively mild climate, with an average temperature throughout the year of 48°F (9°C). Even in winter, the temperature rarely drops far below the freezing point, although it can remain at that chilly level for many days at a time. Cold weather can set in by late October, and January and February are often particularly cold. In February, the average temperature is 34.7°F (1.5°C). In July, the average is 64°F (18°C), but it can sometimes rise to 86°F (30°C) or more.

Annual precipitation in the city is 20 inches (510 mm), with July and August being the wettest months and February the driest.

What to Take

Prague is a modern city with good shops. Nevertheless, if you need special medication, be sure to take it with you. Medicines that can be bought over the counter in your own country may only be available on prescription in the Czech Republic. While most hotels stock electronic adaptors (220V) for laptops, hair driers, etc., it is wise to bring an adaptor with you.

As for clothing, be prepared for all weather, especially in winter, when temperatures range from mild to very cold. Take footwear that can withstand rain and slush. In summer, light slacks or skirts and T-shirts should be sufficient, but be sure to take an umbrella for afternoon showers.

Insurance

Although travel in the Czech Republic will not expose you to unusual dangers, and emergency medical care is free, it is advisable to take out travel insurance to cover other medical expenses, repatriation, and theft. Your travel agent will be able to supply this, but it's best to shop around. If you use a major credit card, such as American Express, to make reservations, you will probably be covered for basic risks and losses, but check the coverage carefully.

Theft & Loss

In the event of theft, inform the police immediately, and be sure to get a copy of the report. Your insurance company will insist on this when processing the claim.

Medical
The Czech Republic provides free emergency care for all foreigners, but charges for non-emergency care, so it is sensible to take out medical insurance. Keep copies of all bills for any medical treatment you receive.

If you do not have health insurance, you can apply for short-term coverage from the company **VZP** (Orlická 4, Prague 3, 221 751 111).

Car
If you are driving your own car to Prague, you should obtain a green card (zelená karta in Czech) from your insurer as proof of motoring insurance before leaving your country of residence. It is usually provided free of charge. You will also need an international driving licence or a licence issued by an E.U. country.

Entry Formalities
You need a valid passport to enter the Czech Republic and stay for up to 90 days. Unless you are an E.U. citizen, the validity of your passport must extend for at least six months from your date of entry.

At present, citizens of the U.S., the E.U., and some other countries do not require visas; Canadians do, however. Check with your travel agent or Czech consulate well in advance

of your journey, as visas cannot be issued at your point of entry.

Further Reading
For cultural context to Prague and the Czech Republic, read the novels of Milan Kundera, Josef Škvorecký, Ivan Klíma, and the late Bohumil Hrabal, whose I Served the King of England is a modern Czech classic. An older Czech classic is The Good Soldier Švejk, a celebrated novel by Jaroslav Hašek set in World War I; for many readers it is the definitive portrayal of the wily Czech character.

The late Václav Havel (1936–2011) was not only the country's president until 2003 but also its most distinguished playwright and essayist. Volumes such as Letters to Olga, written during Havel's 1979–1982 imprisonment, offer insight into Czechoslovakia under the communists. Timothy Garton Ash is the best modern chronicler of the politics of central Europe (The Magic Lantern), and Peter Demetz's Prague in Black and Gold gives a detailed cultural history of the city.

HOW TO GET TO PRAGUE

By Air
Most visitors arrive by air at **Ruzyne,** 12 miles (19 km) from Prague city center. For flight information in English, call 220 113 314 or try the **Czech Airlines (CSA)** website

www.csa.cz. The airport has been modernized, and you are unlikely to meet serious delays at immigration or in the baggage hall.

In addition to Czech Airlines, the Czech national carrier, many airlines provide a regular service from European cities to Prague. There are frequent, though not daily, flights on CSA to Prague from New York and Newark. Many flights from the U.S. connect through British and European airports.

Getting to the City Center
When you book your room, check to see if the hotel offers minibus or limousine service from the airport. If not, **Cedaz** (220 114 296, www.cedaz.cz), a shuttle bus service, will take you to Náměstí Republiky, close to the city center, for 150 Kč ($8.) Tickets are available at the airport newsstand. You can also take local bus 119 to the Metro terminus at Dejvická, from where it is a short ride into the city.

Tickets at the Metro station are 24 Kč ($1.2) for a 30-minute transfer ticket (this allows you to travel on all forms of public transportation) or 32 Kč ($1.5) for a 90-minute ticket. This is the cheapest option by far, but it can be slow and tiring if you have a lot of luggage.

The quickest way to travel into town from the airport is by taxi, but drivers are notoriously dishonest. Be sure to agree on a fare beforehand; expect to pay about 600 Kč ($29) for a one-way trip. Reputable English-speaking companies

include **City Taxi** *(257 257 257)* and **AAA** *(14014)*.

By Train
Prague has four train stations: Nádraži Holešovice, Hlavní nádraži (the main station), Masarykovo nádraži, and Smíchovské nádraži. All are on Metro lines. If you are traveling to Prague by train from another European city, check your ticket to find out your station of arrival.

For train information, call 221 111 122.

By Car
If you drive into Prague, bear in mind that parking in the city center is strictly regulated and signs are not always fully comprehensible to non-Czech readers. Many hotels have parking lots or access to secure parking in the vicinity; expect to pay Kč 200–Kč 350 per day for parking.

By Bus
For U.K.-based travelers, one of the cheapest ways to get to Prague is by bus. **Student Agency** *(www .studentagencybus.com)* offers bus trips six days a week, and the journey takes just under a day. The Prague office can be contacted at 841 101 101, or e-mail info@ studentagencybus.com.

GETTING AROUND

Public Transportation
Prague has an extensive and efficient public transportation system comprising Metro, trams, and buses. Almost all the places you are likely to visit are easily accessible by frequent trams and Metro trains. At night, a limited tram service operates, so you will rarely be completely dependent on taxis.

It is crucial to have a valid ticket before you travel. Plainclothes inspectors check tickets often and will impose an on-the-spot fine of 800 Kč ($39) if you are traveling without a valid ticket. Tickets are valid for up to 30 or 90 minutes only and must be punched as you enter a Metro station or board a tram or bus. Buy tickets from tobacconists and station booking offices. Alternatively, a 24-hour pass costs 110 Kč ($5.5) and a 72-hour pass 310 Kč ($15). Metro and tram maps are displayed at all stations and are available from some station offices.

Metro
There are three lines (see map inside back cover): A (Green), B (Yellow), and C (Red). Trains are frequent and clean; they run from around 5 a.m. to midnight.

Trams
Unlike the Metro, the trams run through the night. But the night trams, lines 51–58, are crowded and less frequent. Line 9 from Wenceslas Square (Václavské náměstí) to Malá Strana is very useful, as is Line 22, which follows a scenic route from the National Theater (Národní divadlo) in Nové Město to the rear of Prague Castle (Pražský hrad).

Buses
Most buses run from Metro terminuses and provide access to suburban destinations, including the airport. You can find bus information on www.dpp.cz or call 800 191 817.

By Taxi
Use taxis as a last resort. Inquire at your hotel about acceptable rates for trips you are planning, then agree with drivers about rates before setting off, or insist that they run their meters (most are disinclined to do so). Discourage overcharging by asking your driver for a receipt with the company's name printed on it. Try **City Taxi** *(257 257 257)* or **AAA** *(14014)*.

On Foot
Prague is a small city—the fastest way to get somewhere in the center is usually by walking. It is a roughly 30-minute stroll from the Castle to the Old Town, and 15 minutes between Old Town Square and the National Museum.

PRACTICAL ADVICE

Cell Phones
European and Australian cell phones will probably work in the Czech Republic, but check with your service provider

before arriving in Prague and be clear about the cost of making calls and using the Internet. Cell phones brought from North America normally use a different frequency and will not work in the Czech Republic unless they have a tri-band frequency option.

Electricity

The Czech electricity supply is 220 volts, and plugs have two round pins. If you bring electrical equipment from the U.S. or the U.K., you will need an adaptor, plus a transformer for 110/120-volt appliances.

Etiquette

It is customary to say "good day" (dobrý den) on entering an office or shop, and to say "goodbye" (na shledanou) on leaving. If you visit a private home, it will be much appreciated if you bring a small gift, such as a bunch of flowers or an item from your own country. In some homes, you will be politely asked to remove your shoes. In pubs and simpler restaurants, you are expected to share tables during busy times.

Money Matters

Czech currency is based on the koruna (plural: koruny), abbreviated to Kč and known in English as crowns. Each crown is divided into 100 hellers, but these coins are no longer in circulation. Money can be changed easily in Prague, where there are dozens of bureaus. Try to avoid changing money at the

airport or border crossings; commission rates are often a steep 5 percent. Beware of bureaus that advertise "no commission"; their rates can be very unfavorable.

Outside major towns and cities, your best bet is to use an ATM. Most banks change currency and charge a minimal fee, but the process can be time-consuming.

Prices in Prague are high compared with the rest of the country. It is hard to find a double room in the city for under 3,000 Kč, which in smaller places would buy you the best suite in town. Similarly, restaurants with French chefs or that cater to foreigners (there are tens of thousands of foreign residents as well as visitors in Prague) charge prices comparable to those of other European cities. Restaurants with a local clientele charge much less, simply because the average Czech cannot afford Berlin or Paris prices.

Major credit cards are accepted in most hotels, restaurants, and stores. Nonetheless, there are exceptions, so it is wise to carry a reasonable amount of Czech currency.

National Holidays

Most castles and some museums are closed on national holidays and the following day. The main national holidays are:
January 1 (New Year's Day)
Easter Sunday
Easter Monday
May 1 (May Day)
May 8 (National Liberation Day)

July 5 (Sts. Cyril and Methodius)
July 6 (Jan Hus Day)
September 28 (St. Václav's Day or Czech Statehood Day)
October 28 (Foundation of the Czechoslovak Republic, 1918)
November 17 (Students' Day)
December 24-26 (Christmas).

Opening Times

Generally, shops, offices, and banks are open from 8 a.m. to 5 p.m. or 9 a.m. to 6 p.m. Some close at lunchtime. Most small shops and banks close on Sunday and holidays, and often on Saturday afternoons. A few shops offer later opening times, and even 24-hour "nonstop" hours. Pharmacies are open from 7:30 a.m. to 6 p.m. on weekdays; some are open 24-hours.

Most restaurants are open for lunch and dinner seven days a week, and do not have the variable day off that is common in France and Germany. Many churches are open all day, especially when they are in use for services, but others have variable opening times. Some are open only during services (these are usually held early in the morning and late afternoon); others close for a period during the day.

Post Offices

Post offices are open Monday to Friday from 8 a.m. to 5 p.m., and on Saturday from 8 a.m. to noon. The main post office in Prague (Jindřišská 14) is open 24 hours. Stamps and phone cards are available from newsstands.

Places of Worship

Many churches are tourist attractions as well as places of worship. The times of services are normally posted on the door and listed in the classified section of *The Prague Post*. Churches do not operate a dress code, except for yarmulkes in synagogues and at the Jewish cemeteries (paper ones are usually available at the synagogues). Many churches also function as concert halls. In some cases, the only way you can see inside a church without paying is to attend a service.

Prague Card

If you are considering visiting several historic sites, galleries, and museums, it may be worth buying the Prague Card. It gives free entry to around 40 major sights, including Prague Castle and the Old Town Hall, and reduced rate entry for more than 30 others. Two-, three-, and four-day options are available (two-day adult card 1,000 Kč/$49; child/student 660 Kč/$32).

A combined Prague Card and Prague Transport Pass gives unlimited travel on all buses, trams, Metros, and trains in the city as well (two-day adult card 1,260 Kč/$61; child/student 910 Kč/$44). You can order the Card online and pick it up on arrival or buy it at various locations in the city (*www.praguecard.com*).

Rest Rooms

Public rest rooms are usually clearly marked "WC"; a small charge (around 5 Kč/25 cents) is levied for admission and some sheets of toilet paper. Standards vary, but most rest rooms are clean and properly maintained. Women should look for the words *Dámy* or *Ženy;* men for *Páni* or *Muži*. However, be aware that *paní* with the accent on the "i" means "women" and is sometimes used on WC doors. Additional facilities, sometimes free and better maintained, are available at many Metro stations, department stores, museums, restaurants, and cafés.

Safety

There was a time when an evening stroll down Wenceslas Square could well be ruined by the gangs of pickpockets who roamed the area. Those days are over, and Prague is no more dangerous than any large European city.

Pickpockets are still at work in the Metro, and on trams and at tram stops. Trams 22 and 23 are popular with tourists— and with pickpockets. Tourist attractions such as the Charles Bridge (Karlův most) are also prime spots. Speaking English or German can be enough to draw attention to yourself. Keep wallets in front pockets; fasten purses and hold them close to your body. Similarly, be vigilant when withdrawing cash from ATMs at night: Don't allow

yourself to be distracted by "helpful" strangers.

Unsavory characters, including drug addicts, often congregate at the main train station, the park in front of it, and the Florenc bus terminal, especially late at night. Take care if you find yourself in these locations.

Telephones

If you don't have your own cell phone (see pp. 174–175), the easiest way to make phone calls, both local and international, is to use a phone card, which can be bought from newsstands and grocery stores. Using the phone in your hotel room can prove extremely expensive, especially when making international calls.

Time Differences

The Czech Republic runs on CET (Central European Time), one hour ahead of GMT (Greenwich Mean Time), six hours ahead of New York, and nine hours ahead of Los Angeles. Clocks change for daylight saving on the last Sunday in March (one hour forward), and go back one hour on the last Sunday in October.

Tipping

In general, Czechs do not tip, but they do round up the bill in restaurants. For example, if your bill comes to 282 Kč, you might hand your waiter 300 Kč in notes and tell him or her to keep the change. If it comes to 235 Kč, you could ask for 50 Kč back.

Travelers with Disabilities

Special provisions for the disabled are still the exception rather than the rule in Prague, but the city's hotels, restaurants, and museums are becoming increasingly aware of the need to cater to such special needs. The main problem faced by people with disabilities is using public transportation, as it's impossible to get a wheelchair onto a tram. The **Prague Wheelchair Association** (*Benediktská 6, Staré Město, Prague, 224 821 210*) publishes *Accessible Prague*, a guide to facilities for the disabled. The travel agency **Accessible Prague** also provides assistance at www .accessibleprague.com.

Visitor Information

Information bureaus are readily identifiable by a large, bright green, lowercase letter i. Some bureaus are very useful, and can assist with hotel bookings. Others are essentially glorified sales outlets for postcard producers. Overall, however, they are mines of information, offering maps, booklets, and verbal guidance.

The main visitor information centers are located at the main station, Hlavní nádraži (*Wilsonova*), and in the Old Town Hall (Staroměstské náměstí). If you are planning an excursion out of Prague, it is worth visiting the latter, where staff can give you the opening times of all castles and museums throughout the Czech Republic. The Prague information center has a useful website at www.pis.cz.

EMERGENCIES

Embassies

United States Embassy
Tržiště 15, Prague 1, 257 530 663. Open Mon.–Fri. 8 a.m.– 4:30 p.m. (consular hours 9 a.m.–noon).

Canadian Embassy
Muchova 6, Prague 6, 272 101 800. Open Mon.–Fri. 8 a.m.–4 p.m.

British Embassy *Thunovská 14, Prague 1, 257 402 111. Open Mon.–Fri. 9 a.m.–noon.*

Emergency Phone Numbers

Police 112
Fire 112
Ambulance 112
Automobile emergencies 1230

Health

If you think you need a doctor during your stay, consult your hotel reception staff, who will be able to direct you to an English-speaking doctor or arrange for one to visit you in your room. For minor ailments, it's often best to go to a pharmacy (*lékárna*), where, if language barriers can be overcome, you can obtain free advice and inexpensive medicines.

Most pharmacies close at 6 p.m. but the following are open 24 hours:
Palackého 5, Prague 1, near Můstek Metro station, 224 946 982
Belgická 37, Prague 2, near Náměstí Míru Metro station, 222 519 731
Štefánikova 6, Prague 5, near Anděl, 257 320 918

The recommended clinic for foreigners is the **Na Homolce Hospital** (*Roentgenova 2, Smíchov, Prague 5, 257 271 111*), which has English-speaking staff. If you have a dental emergency while visiting Prague, go to **Palackého Poliklinika** (*Palackého 5, 224 946 981*).

The **Canadian Medical Center** is open 24 hours (*Veleslavínská 1, Prague 6, 235 360 133; after hours 724 300 301 (general practice) and 724 300 303 (pediatrician), www.cmcpraha.cz.*)

Lost Property

The city's central lost property office is at Karolíny Světlé 5, Prague 1, 224 235 085. Open weekdays 8 a.m.–noon, 12:30 p.m.–5:30 p.m.

If you lose your credit card while in Prague, telephone the relevant provider as soon as possible:
American Express, 222 412 241
Visa/Eurocard/Mastercard, 800 111 055
Diners Club, 267 197 450

HOTELS

Prague hotels have improved by leaps and bounds in the last decade or two, and there is now a good range of accommodations to suit all tastes and budgets. You will find character-filled older-style hotels with antique furniture and old-fashioned decor, some in former palaces, and a plethora of surprisingly affordable designer hotels with sleek furnishings, hi-tech gadgetry, and contemporary color schemes.

Accommodations

Prague has hundreds of hotels and guesthouses, but at certain times of the year—especially summer and Christmas—a room is difficult to find. It's best to make reservations well in advance. Czech tourist offices provide lists of hotels in Prague.

Standards are generally high in the Czech capital. Almost all rooms have bathrooms and basic facilities such as telephones and televisions. While you can assume rooms will be comfortable and clean, don't always expect light, airy rooms with modern furnishings: Decor and furniture tend to be traditional, which means dark and heavy. That said, a growing number of boutique hotels offer a more contemporary style.

Prices should include all taxes, but it's sensible to check this before making a reservation. The room rate often includes breakfast. Major credit cards are accepted in all but the smallest hotels.

Price ranges indicated in the listings below are official "rack rates"—what you pay if you walk in and ask the rate. Except during the high season, it is usually possible to negotiate a discount if you reserve in advance, especially at some of the luxury hotels that have high overhead costs, or out of season, when occupancy rates are lower.

There is little clear difference between a hotel and a pension. A pension will usually be family-run, and it may not have a reception desk; guests are provided with a key to the front door as if to a private house.

If you are planning to stay a week or more, it is worth considering a "residence" or private accommodations. A residence provides a fully furnished apartment, often centrally located, with cooking facilities. Prices vary enormously, depending on location, the quality of facilities, and the degree of privacy.

A few agencies specialize in locating accommodations in private apartments. Try **Ave Travel** at the main train station (*Hlavní nádraží, 251 551 011,* *www.avetravel.cz*) or the **Stop City** agency (*Vinohradská 24, 222 251 234, www.stopcity.com*).

Organization

The hotels listed here have been grouped by area. They are then listed alphabetically by price category. The postal address Prague 1 covers the central part of the city— Hradčany, Malá Strana, and Staré Město. Visitors with disabilities should check facilities with establishments.

Price Range

An indication of the cost of a double room in the high season is given by **$** signs.

$$$$$ More than $200
$$$$ $130–$200
$$$ $80–$130
$$ $50–$80
$ Less than $50

Text Symbols

🛈 *No. of Guest Rooms*
🚋 *Public Transportation*
🅿 *Parking* 🛗 *Elevator*
❄ *Air-conditioning*
🚭 *Nonsmoking* 🏊 *Outdoor Pool*
🏊 *Indoor Pool* 💪 *Health Club*
💳 *Credit Cards*

STARÉ MĚSTO

The narrow streets of Staré Město have many of Prague's most exciting hotels, including some in grand palaces or art nouveau mansions.

■ BUDDHA BAR HOTEL
$$$$$
JAKUBSKÁ 8
PRAGUE 1
TEL 221 776 300
FAX 221 776 310
www.buddha-bar-hotel.cz
Leave Old Prague behind for a taste of modern orientalism at this hotel version of Paris's hyper-hip nightclub. Dark woods, red accents, low lighting, incense, and Buddha beat music add to its mystical, romantic charm. Turndown service includes chocolates and an orchid, and also a "pillow" menu. If you don't stay overnight, come for a meal at Siddartha café, with its Asian fusion cuisine, or a drink at the super chic bar.

ⓘ 39 🚇 Náměstí Republiky
🚊 📺 🌐 All major cards

■ KEMPINSKI HYBERNSKÁ PRAGUE
$$$$$
HYBERNSKÁ 12
PRAGUE 1
TEL 226 226 111
www.kempinski.com
Housed in a retrofitted 15th-century baroque palace just steps from the Powder Tower and Municipal Hall, this business hotel on the edge of Staré Město features contemporary decor in generously sized rooms that

are more like apartments than hotel rooms, with a separate bedroom, living area, and kitchenette. You can expect top-notch service.

ⓘ 75 🚇 Náměstí Republiky
🚊 🚌 📺 🌐 All major cards

■ PAŘÍŽ
$$$$–$$$$$
U OBECNÍHO DOMU 1
PRAGUE 1
TEL 222 195 195
FAX 224 225 475
www.hotel-pariz.cz
This gorgeous secessionist hotel was renovated to combine comfort and beauty. Public rooms include the Café de Paris, with its art nouveau light fittings. Look for the lovely ironwork on the staircase.

ⓘ 94 🚇 Náměstí Republiky
🅿 🚊 📺 🌐 All major cards

■ UNGELT
$$$$–$$$$$
MALÁ ŠTUPARTSKÁ 646-7
PRAGUE 1
TEL 221 771 011
FAX 221 771 090
www.ungelt.cz
Situated behind the Týn Church, the Ungelt offers spacious apartments with a kitchenette. Some have two bedrooms, sleeping four.

ⓘ 10 🚇 Náměstí Republiky
🚊 🌐 All major cards

■ CENTRAL
$$$$
RYBNÁ 8
PRAGUE 1
TEL 222 317 220
FAX 222 315 386
www.central-prague.com
Built in 1931, the Central, near Náměstí Republiky,

was renovated in the 1990s. Rooms are simply furnished. The best and priciest, on the top floors, have balconies with views over the medieval rooftops. There is an attractive lobby bar.

ⓘ 68 🚇 Náměstí Republiky
🅿 🚊 📺 🌐 MC, V

■ RESIDENCE ŘETĚZOVÁ
$$–$$$$$
ŘETĚZOVÁ 9
PRAGUE 1
TEL 222 221 800
www.retezova.com
This renovated 15th-century building in the center of Staré Město offers a range of accommodations in self-catering units that incorporate many of the building's original features. This is a good choice if you are staying in Prague for more than just a few days.

ⓘ 9 🚇 Staroměstská
🚊 🌐 All major cards

■ HOTEL JOSEF
$$$
RYBNÁ 20
PRAGUE 1
TEL 221 700 111
FAX 221 700 999
www.hoteljosef.com
This designer hotel, created by Czech-U.K. architect Eva Jiřičná, has won much critical praise since it opened in 2002. The rooms are small, but the glass walls and interior decor with clean lines create a sense of minimalist chic, and the sharp service and affordability make it an attractive choice.

ⓘ 109 🚇 Náměstí Republiky
🅿 🚊 📺 🌐 AE, MC, V

■ LIPPERT HOTEL

$$$
MIKULÁŠSKÁ 19/2
PRAGUE 1
TEL 224 232 250
FAX 224 232 249
www.hotel-lippert.cz

Considering its location right on Staroměstské náměstí, this hotel is a cozy, classy, old-fashioned option with competitive rates. Rafters, wooden floors, and cushy sofas fill out this tastefully modernized 14th-century building. Its summer terrace fronts the square.

🚹 12 🚇 Staromestská
♠ All major cards

■ U ČERVENÉ ŽIDLE

$$$
LILIOVÁ 4
PRAGUE 1
TEL 296 180 018
www.redchairhotel.com

This guesthouse, whose name means the Red Chair, exudes charm. It occupies a 15th-century building with many period features. The rooms, which range from singles to quads, have minimal but tidy furnishings and all have private baths. Breakfast is a continental-style buffet.

🚹 15 🚇 Můstek
🅿 🚬 ♠ AE, MC, V

■ UNITAS

$$$
BARTOLOMĚJSKÁ 9
PRAGUE 1
TEL 224 230 533
FAX 224 230 532
www.unitas.cz

This is a clean but spartan budget choice, with twin and triple rooms and some dormitory-style rooms in what was originally a convent and later the headquarters of the state secret police. All bathroom facilities are shared and the rooms are hardly spacious, but the beds are clean and comfortable, and the location, just a short walk from Charles Bridge and Old Town, is good.

🚹 34 🚇 Národní třída
🅿 🚬 ♠ None

JOSEFOV

There are fewer hotels in the former Jewish quarter than in the other central areas, but hip shops, cocktail bars, and restaurants pack the elegant buildings, creating a lively atmosphere in the evening.

■ INTERCONTINENTAL

$$$$$
NÁMĚSTÍ CURIEOVÝCH 43/5
PRAGUE 1
TEL 296 631 111
FAX 224 811 216
www.icprague.com

A number of international chains have hotels in Prague, but this has the best location: On the river, a few minutes' walk from Josefov. As well as having all the restaurant and business facilities one expects from a hotel of this caliber and price (most notably the rooftop restaurant, *Zlatá Praha*), the hotel has wheelchair access and a Casa del Habano cigar shop.

🚹 364 🚇 Staroměstská
🅿 🚬 ♠ All major cards

MALÁ STRANA & HRADČANY

Hotels abound in Malá Strana below Prague Castle and around Charles Bridge, making it one of the most popular places to stay.

■ ALCHYMIST GRAND HOTEL & SPA

$$$$$
TRŽIŠTĚ 19
PRAGUE 1
TEL 251 286 011
FAX 251 286 017
www.alchymisthotel.com

This palatial pile next to the American embassy features kingly rooms with timbered ceilings, a gourmet restaurant serving continental cuisine, and a pool and spa specializing in massage, aromatherapy, and wraps. Service is top-notch, with a concierge standing by to help with hard-to-acquire event tickets and tips on what's going on in the city.

🚹 46 🚇 Malostranská
🅿 🚬 ♠ All major cards

■ HOFFMEISTER

$$$$$
POD BRUSKOU 7
PRAGUE 1
TEL 251 017 111
FAX 251 017 120
www.hoffmeister.cz

The Hoffmeister, Prague's only Relais & Châteaux group member, offers luxury and excellent service. The rooms are very richly furnished, with heavy draperies, but the location along a busy tramline beneath the castle may not be ideal. There's a fine and tasteful restaurant, the Ada, and the terrace is delightful in summer.

(i) 41 **[M]** *Malostranská*
P **[⊟]** **[◫]** **[◈]** *All major cards*

■ **SAVOY**
$$$$$
KEPLEROVA 6
PRAGUE 1
TEL 224 302 430
FAX 224 302 128
www.savoyhotel.cz
This is an art nouveau building near the Strahov Monastery. Its elegant public rooms include a lobby bar, with curved banquettes, where you can order a wide range of snacks and light meals, and the glass-roofed Hradčany restaurant. The bedrooms are among the largest in the city, with complimentary minibars and spacious marble bathrooms. Guests have free use of the fitness center. The hotel is extremely popular with celebrities, but the distance from the city center may be a disadvantage for most visitors to Prague.

(i) 61 **[M]** *Malostranská* **P** **[⊟]**
[◫] **[◉]** **[◫]** **[◈]** *All major cards*

■ **U TŘÍ PŠTROSŮ**
$$$$$
DRAŽICKÉHO NÁMĚSTÍ 12
PRAGUE 1
TEL 257 288 888
FAX 257 533 217
www.utripstrosu.cz
The Three Ostriches, in the shadow of the Charles Bridge, is one of Prague's best-established inns. It was the city's first coffeehouse,

and until the 1960s was run by the Dundr family, who regained possession in the 1990s. The rooms look a little dated but the public areas retain precious Renaissance features including a painted wooden ceiling. The U Tří Pštrosů restaurant offers a good selection of fish, game dishes, such as leg of boar with rosehip sauce, traditional Czech dishes, and ostrich specialties. There's a cheaper lunchtime selection.

(i) 18 **[M]** *Malostranská*
P **[◈]** *All major cards*

■ **THE GREEN LOBSTER**
$$$$–$$$$$
NERUDOVA 224/42
PRAGUE 1
TEL 257 532 158
FAX 257 531 120
www.garzottohotels.cz
Original 14th-century features such as carved ceilings and wooden floors survive in this former mansion turned comfortable hotel/residence. Gilt edged furniture (including some four-poster beds) and rich textiles in vibrant reds and gold add to the palatial impression. The spacious Executive rooms have the finest period features and front-facing views.

(i) 19 **[M]** *Malostranská*
P **[⊟]** **[◫]** **[◈]** *All major cards*

■ **U ZLATÉ STUDNĚ**
$$$$–$$$$$
U ZLATÉ STUDNĚ 4
PRAGUE 1
TEL 257 011 213
FAX 257 533 320
www.goldenwell.cz
Tucked away in a quiet

cul-de-sac beneath the castle, this elegant 16th-century mansion, once the property of Emperor Rudolf II and astronomer Tycho Brahe, has been skillfully converted into one of the best hotels in Prague. All rooms are individually furnished to the highest standard, with a Jacuzzi in every bathroom. The equally luxurious restaurant offers a short menu of dishes that blend different European cuisines. The decor is essentially modern, and in summer a roof terrace next to the Ledebur Gardens has what must be the best view over Malá Strana.

(i) 19 **[M]** *Malostranská*
P **[◫]** **[◈]** *All major cards*

■ **THE AUGUSTINE**
$$$$
LETENSKÁ 12
PRAGUE 1
TEL 266 112 422
FAX 266 112 234
www.theaugustine.com
Occupying a former monastery and doubling as one of the city's most venerated beer halls, this atmospheric hotel features a fine dining restaurant that combines fresh designer style with classic Old Europe woodwork and high ceilings. Rooms, some of which have spectacular views, feature elegant but comfortable modernist designs. The hotel spa offers a wide range of pampering treatments.

(i) 101 **[M]** *Malostranská*
P **[⊟]** **[◫]** **[◈]** *All major cards*

■ DŮM U VELKĚ BOTY
$$$$
VALAŠSKÁ 30
PRAGUE 1
TEL/FAX 257 532 088
www.dumuvelkeboty.cz
The "House at the Big Boot"
occupies a 17th-century
burgher's house overlooking
the German Embassy on a
quiet square. Family-run, it is
delightfully quirky with wooden
beams, stone staircases, and
lots of period details. All the
rooms have private facilities,
though some have only a
shower, and there is one suite
with a living room and kitchen.
Children under the age of 10
stay free if they share a room
with their parents.
① 12 🚇 *Malostranská* 🐾 *None*

■ SAX
$$$$
JÁNSKÝ VRŠEK 3
PRAGUE 1
TEL 257 531 268
FAX 257 534 101
www.hotelsax.cz
If old palaces don't float your
boat, this discreet hotel on
a quiet square off Vlašská
in the heart of Malá Strana
might be just the thing. The
retro-style rooms with their
bold wallpapers and sleek
furnishings have won design
awards, and the stylish lobby
bar in a courtyard atrium is
decorated with modern art.
Several rooms look over the
tiled rooftops of the old city
center, and there is a view of
the castle from the terrace.
① 22 🚇 *Malostranská*
P 😄 🐾 *All major cards*

■ U PÁVA
$$$$
U LUŽICKÉHO SEMINÁŘE 32
PRAGUE 1
TEL 257 533 360
www.hotel-upava.cz
U Páva is located on a quiet
square just a short distance
from the Charles Bridge.
The dark wood furnishings,
extravagant frescoes, and
heavy drapery are not to
everyone's taste, and can
seem a little gloomy, but
the rooms are large and
sumptuous. It is worth
investigating the suites,
which are only slightly more
expensive than the de luxe
double rooms and come
with a fireplace—a nice touch
in winter.
① 27 🚇 *Malostranská*
P 😄 🐾 *AE, MC, V*

■ ZLATÁ HVĚZDA
$$$$
NERUDOVA 48
PRAGUE 1
TEL 257 532 867
FAX 257 533 624
www.hotelgoldenstar.cz
The grand Zlatá Hvězda
in the heart of Malá Strana
occupies a magnificent
1730s' baroque building. It
was reconstructed in 2000,
but original features such as
the ornate plasterwork and
beams were retained. The
rooms vary in size, but all
have period wooden furniture,
modern comforts, and good
views over Malá Strana or
the castle.
① 26 🚇 *Malostranská*
P 😄 🐾 *AE, MC, V*

■ PENSION DIENTZENHOFER
$$$
NOSTICOVA 2
PRAGUE 1
TEL 257 311 319
FAX 257 320 888
www.dientzenhofer.cz
The birthplace of architect
Kilián Ignátz Dientzenhofer,
close to Kampa Island, now
flourishes as a small hotel
and restaurant. The location
is appealing and quiet, but
the rooms, although quite
spacious, could do with a
makeover. There is wheelchair
access, a pleasant garden
terrace, and WiFi in the
public areas.
① 9 🚇 *Malostranská*
P 😄 🐾 *All major cards*

■ NH PRAGUE
$$$
MOZARTOVA 261/1
PRAGUE 5
TEL 257 151 111
FAX 257 153 131
www.nh-hotels.com
Pink and starkly modern, this
option is not to everyone's
taste, but it is a popular
business hotel and useful for
travelers with cars, because
access is easy and there is
ample parking. Moreover,
prices are fair. The rooms
have modern furnishings
and the beds have thick
mattresses and luxurious
duvets. A special cable
car leads to the "Executive
Building," which has a lovely
outdoor terrace with superb
views over the city.
① 434 🚇 *Anděl*
P 😄 🚫 🎭 🐾 *All major cards*

TRAVEL ESSENTIALS

NOVÉ MĚSTO

Centering on Wenceslas Square, the Nové Město has a more spacious feel than Staré Město and Malá Strana and still offers easy access to the main sights.

■ JALTA
$$$$$
VÁCLAVSKÉ NÁMĚSTÍ 45
PRAGUE 1
TEL 222 822 111
FAX 222 822 833
www.jalta.cz
Built in the 1950s as a showpiece of communist architecture, Jalta has metamorphosed into a comfortable four-star hotel with well-appointed and spacious rooms. An unusual feature is the former nuclear fallout shelter discovered beneath the building; the hotel provides tours for guests and the public. The Como Restaurant serves Mediterranean, Asian, and Czech specialties and includes a bar and terrace overlooking Wenceslas Square.
🛈 94 🚇 Můstek
🅿 🔄 🌊 AE, DC, JCB, MC, V

■ AMBASSADOR ZLATÁ HUSA
$$$$-$$$$$
VÁCLAVSKÉ NÁMĚSTÍ 5-7
PRAGUE 1
TEL 224 193 111
FAX 224 230 620
www.ambassador.cz
The Ambassador's location on Wenceslas Square is hard to beat, and the guest rooms are comfortable and well equipped. The public rooms lack atmosphere—though there is an impressive art nouveau banquet room—and some of the furnishings are rather dated. The hotel adjoins the nightclub and casino.
🛈 160 🚇 Můstek
🔄 🌊 🚫 🌊 All major cards

■ CITY HOTEL MORAN
$$$$-$$$$$
NA MORÁNI 15
PRAGUE 2
TEL 224 915 208
FAX 224 920 625
www.bestwestern.com
Now part of the Best Western stable, this is an attractive 19th-century building with rooms that are spacious and well equipped, if a little functional. Situated near the river, just off Charles Square, it is a comfortable choice in this part of town.
🛈 57 🚇 Karlovo náměstí
🅿 🔄 🌊 🌊 All major cards

■ PALACE PRAHA
$$$$-$$$$$
PANSKÁ 12
PRAGUE 1
TEL 224 093 111
FAX 224 221 240
www.palacehotel.cz
This 1906 secessionist building is perfectly located just off Wenceslas Square. One of Prague's first luxury hotels, it is still holding its own. It is expensive, but has personality, and is very well equipped and effortlessly comfortable. Many of the rooms are individually decorated; all are stylish, with fine-quality fabrics for curtains and bedspreads. A cozy wood-paneled dining room with a piano and fireplace helps make it an ideal choice for a mid-winter stay.
🛈 124 🚇 Můstek
🅿 🌊 🌊 🌊 All major cards

■ HOTEL ELITE
$$$
OSTROVNÍ 32
PRAGUE 1
TEL 211 156 500
FAX 211 156 787
www.hotelelite.cz
This former baroque barracks represents one of Prague's best deals, especially considering the wealth of period details, the antique furniture in the public areas, and the individual decor of each room. The hotel has an excellent reputation for service and is situated just within easy walking distance of Staré Město.
🛈 76 🚇 Národní třída
🅿 🔄 🌊 All major cards

■ CITY BELL
$-$$
BELGICKÁ 10
PRAGUE 2
TEL/FAX 222 522 422
www.hotelcitybell.cz
The City Bell, a five-minute walk from Náměstí Miru, is one of the few bargains in the city center. The rooms are large and bright, but basic and sparsely furnished. The cheaper rooms have separate, shared bathrooms. Service is exceptionally helpful.
🛈 24 🚇 Náměstí Miru
🅿 🔄 🌊 All major cards

LANGUAGE GUIDE

TRAVEL ESSENTIALS

General Conversation
Good day/Hello *dobrý den*
Goodbye *na shledanou*
Please *prosím*
Thank you *děkuji*
Yes *ano*
No *ne*
Good/OK *dobře*
Sorry/Excuse me *promiňte*
Where is? *kde je?*
When? *kdy?*
Why? *proč?*
Large/Small *velký/malý*
More/Less *více/méně*
Hot/Cold *horký/studený*
Here/There *tady/tam*
Right/Left *vpravo/vlevo*
Straight ahead *jděte přímo*

Signs
Vchod *entrance*
Východ *exit*
Otevřeno *open*
Zavřeno *closed*
Pozor *take care*
Toalety *rest rooms*
Muži/Páni *men/gentlemen*
Ženy/Dámy *women/ladies*

Time
Today *dnes*
Tomorrow *zítra*
Yesterday *včera*
Morning *ráno*
Afternoon *odpoledne*
Evening *večer*
Night *noc*

Shopping
Cash desk *pokladna*
Post office *pošta*
Bank *banka*
Grocery store *potraviny*
Chemist *lékárna*
Expensive/Cheap *drahý/ levný*
How much is it? *Kolik to stojí?*

Transportation
Airport *letiště*
Railway station *nádraží*
Bus station *autobusové nádraží*
Metro station *stanice metra*
Airplane *letadlo*
Train *vlak*
Bus *autobus*
Tram *tramvaj*
Seat *místo/sedadlo*
Ticket *lístek*
One-way *jednosměrný*
Return *zpáteční*

Geography & Places
Tourist office *informační centrum*
Theater *divadlo*
Garden *zahrada*
Church *kostel*
Museum *muzeum*
Bridge *most*
Avenue *třída*
Square *náměstí*
Street *ulice*
Castle *hrad*
Château *zámek*
Mountain *hora*
River *řeka*

Hotels
Hotel *hotel*
Room *pokoj*
Breakfast *snídaně*
Key *klíč*
Reservation *rezervace*
Toilet *toaleta*
Bath *koupelna*
Shower *sprcha*

Emergencies
Help! *pomoc!*
Doctor *doktor/lékař*
Dentist *zubař*
Hospital *nemocnice*
Police station *policejní stanice*

Numbers
1 *jeden*
2 *dva*
3 *tří*
4 *čtyři*
5 *pět*
6 *šest*
7 *sedm*
8 *osm*
9 *devět*
10 *deset*
15 *patnáct*
20 *dvacet*
25 *dvacet pět*
50 *padesát*
100 *sto*
1000 *tisíc*
1,000,000 *milión*

Days of the Week
Monday *pondělí*
Tuesday *úterý*
Wednesday *středa*
Thursday *čtvrtek*
Friday *pátek*
Saturday *sobota*
Sunday *neděle*

Months of the Year & Seasons
January *leden*
February *únor*
March *březen*
April *duben*
May *květen*
June *červen*
July *červenec*
August *srpen*
September *září*
October *říjen*
November *listopad*
December *prosinec*

Spring *jaro*
Summer *léto*
Fall *podzim*
Winter *zima*

MENU **READER**

General Terms
restaurant *restaurace*
menu *jídelní lístek*
table *stůl*
lunch *oběd*
dinner *večeře*
appetizer *předkrm*
main meal *hlavní jídlo*
side dish *příloha*
dessert *moučník*
wine list *nápojový lístek*
the bill *účet*

Basics
bread *chléb*
butter *máslo*
cheese *sýr*
cream *smetana*
eggs *vejce*
fruit *ovoce*
meat *maso*
pepper *pepř*
salt *sůl*
soup *polévka*
sugar *cukr*
vegetables *zelenina*

Meats
bažant pheasant
drůbež poultry
hovězí beef
husa goose
játra liver
kachna duck
klobása sausage
králík rabbit
krocan turkey
kuře chicken
párek Vienna sausage
šunka ham
telecí veal
vepřové pork
vepřové koleno pork knee
vepřový řízek schnitzel

Seafood
kapr carp
krevety prawns
pstruh trout
ryby fish
treska cod
tuna tuňák
uzený losos smoked salmon

Side Dishes
bramborová kaše mashed potatoes
brambory potatoes
hranolky french fries
knedlíky dumplings
rýže rice
salát salad

Fruit
ananas pineapple
banán banana
citrón lemon
hrozny grapes
hruška pear
jablko apple
jahody strawberries
pomeranč orange
rozinky raisins

Vegetables
česnek garlic
cibule onion
hrášek peas
květák cauliflower
mrkev/karotka carrot
okurka cucumber
rajčata tomatoes
špenát spinach
žampiony mushrooms
zelí cabbage

Other
chlebíček open sandwiches
omeleta omelette
smažený sýr fried cheese

Desserts
buchty curd cakes
čokoláda chocolate
dort cake
palačinky pancakes
závin strudel
zmrzlina ice cream

Drinks
voda water
minerální voda mineral water
  nešumivá still
  šumivá sparkling
mléko milk
čaj tea
káva coffee
pomerančový džus orange juice
červené víno red wine
bílé víno white wine
pivo beer

Pronunciation Guide
Most English-speakers find pronunciation a problem, but the system of accents should make it clear. Acute accents (or in the case of "u," ů) lengthen the vowel. The stress usually falls on the first syllable. There are some clear differences from "English-style" pronunciation:

á = as in far
c = *ts* as in cats
č = *ch* as in cheek
ch = *ch* as in loch
ě = *ye* as in yet
é = *ea* as in pear
í and ý = *ee* as in see
j = *y* as in yawn
ň = *ny* as in banyan
r = as in bourgeois (combined rolled r and ž sound)
š = *sh* as in shabby
ú and ů = *oo* as in zoo
y = *i* as in fit
ž = *zh* sound as in measure

INDEX

INDEX

INDEX

INDEX

Walking Prague

Published by the National Geographic Society
Gary E. Knell, **President and Chief Executive Officer**
John M. Fahey, Jr., **Chairman of the Board**
Declan Moore, **Chief Media Officer**
Chris Johns, **Chief Content Officer**
Keith Bellows, **Senior Vice President and Editor in Chief,**
    National Geographic Travel Media

Prepared by the Book Division
Hector Sierra, **Senior Vice President and General Manager**
Janet Goldstein, **Senior Vice President and Editorial Director**
Jonathan Halling, **Creative Director**
Marianne R. Koszorus, **Design Director**
Barbara A. Noe, **Senior Editor**
Elisa Gibson, **Art Director**
R. Gary Colbert, **Production Director**
Mike Horenstein, **Production Manager**
Jennifer A. Thornton, **Director of Managing Editorial**
Susan S. Blair, **Director of Photography**
Meredith C. Wilcox, **Director, Administration and Rights**
    Clearance
Marshall Kiker, **Associate Managing Editor**
Judith Klein, **Production Editor**
Marlena Serviss, **Contributor**
Katie Olsen, **Design Production Specialist**
Nicole Miller, **Design Production Assistant**
Bobby Barr, **Manager, Production Services**

Created by Toucan Books Ltd
Ellen Dupont, **Editorial Director**
Helen Douglas-Cooper, **Editor**
Dave Jones, **Designer**
Sharon Southren, **Picture Research**
Petr Hejný, **Editorial Support**
Merritt Cartographic, **Maps**
Marion Dent, **Proofreader**
Marie Lorimer, **Indexer**

The information in this book has been carefully checked and to the best of our knowledge is accurate. However, details are subject to change, and the National Geographic Society cannot be responsible for such changes, or for errors or omissions. Assessments of sites, hotels, and restaurants are based on the author's subjective opinions, which do not necessarily reflect the publisher's opinion.

The National Geographic Society is one of the world's largest nonprofit scientific and educational organizations. Its mission is to inspire people to care about the planet. Founded in 1888, the Society is member supported and offers a community for members to get closer to explorers, connect with other members and help make a difference. The Society reaches more than 450 million people worldwide each month through *National Geographic* and other magazines; National Geographic Channel television documentaries; music; radio; films; books; DVDs; maps; exhibitions; live events; school publishing programs; interactive media; and merchandise. National Geographic reflects the world through its magazines, television programs, films, music and radio, books, DVDs, maps, exhibitions, live events, school publishing programs, interactive media, and merchandise. National Geographic has funded more than 10,000 scientific research, conservation, and exploration projects and supports an education program promoting geography literacy. For more information, visit www.nationalgeographic.com.

For more information, please call 1-800-NGS LINE (647-5463) or write to the following address:

National Geographic Society
1145 17th Street N.W.
Washington, D.C. 20036-4688 U.S.A.

For information about special discounts for bulk purchases, please contact National Geographic Books Special Sales: ngspecsales@ngs.org

For rights or permissions inquiries, please contact National Geographic Books Subsidiary Rights: ngbookrights@ngs.org

ISBN: 978-1-4262-1470-7

Printed in Hong Kong
14/THK/1